D0425274

Who Trusts in God

Who Trusts in God

MUSINGS ON THE MEANING OF PROVIDENCE

ALBERT C. OUTLER

New York OXFORD UNIVERSITY PRESS 1968

Library of Congress Catalogue Card Number 68-17616
Printed in the United States of America

Who trusts in God, a strong abode
In heaven and earth possesses . . .

JOACHIM OF MAGDEBURG
(1571)

To

My Father and Mother,

Who taught me the Christian style of life,

Mostly by living it,

In Grateful Memory

Preface

This little book is a revision of the Sprunt Lectures for 1967 at Union Theological Seminary (Richmond). The choice of their topic was largely predetermined. For a long time now, "the problem of God" has been front and center on the theological stage, what with the fading of neo-orthodox fideism and the climax of the experiment in the reduction of theology to anthropology, and it is still far from any real stability. Thus, I felt I had to talk about *theo*logy. And, since the basic theme of the current radical theologies is the *absence* of God, it occurred to me that it might be interesting to try to say something about his *presence*—in the world and in human history. This, however, was the *intent* of the traditional doctrines of "providence." And so the doctrine of providence was conceived of as a sort of test-case: if a reasonably honest, but freely revised, version of the traditional affirmations of God's provident presence could be rendered at all credible to "moderns," the case for *theo*logy would be strengthened by so much and the self-evidence of the claims of religious humanism might be brought into some fruitful doubt. I was—and still am—very much aware of the hazards of any such project and the penalties for failure. It is unfashionable to the point of embarrassment nowadays for a theologian, avowedly not a fundamentalist, even to propose an affirmative restatement of any "traditional belief" (the phrase itself is prejudged). But, a safer course would have been duller and, besides, it is actually the case that I do believe what I have here affirmed.

Once the topic was decided on, the outline came easy. As a historian with a passionate concern for the carryover of history into constructive theology (or a theologian who comes at systematic questions historically), I had to begin with an attempt to set the issues involved in their historical perspective. This is the undertaking of the first chapter. Then, allowing that the question of "divine intervention" is the crux of most "modern" rejections of the idea of providence, the second chapter had to consider the prior question of the ultimate environment of "nature" and "history" and then to ask just how impervious ("closed") these orders of existence really are (and impervious to what?).

From here the line of argument was clear enough, even if the arguments may not be: the question of divine "providence" and "presence" (ch. 3) and a *theologia crucis* as a "lived solution" to the problem of evil (ch. 4). Finally, lest the point be missed that the validation of any doctrine of God's providence is in its practical import for *humane living in this world*, the concluding chapter points to the fruitage of faith in a Christian "style of life." Some such expository pattern—perspective, restatement, practical application—is meant to involve the reader in his own ponderings on the warrants of his own faith.

But the decision to turn the lectures into a book was a reluctant one. Most public addresses—mine, at any rate—make better listening than reading. In the two-way traffic of the spoken word, the strong points of an argument can be made to stand out. In the one-way traffic of cold print on a flat page, its strengths and weaknesses lie equally exposed. The historian notices the historical generalizations that might be supportable but that are not here supported. The philosopher sees the theses that might be arguable but that are not here argued out. The lover of lean and graceful language may find the rhetoric florid. And the professional theologian will blanch a bit at so reckless an exposure of personal belief and positive affirmation. I feel all of these misgivings in myself and, as I have proofread the manuscript, have been able to foresee reviews that will rightly complain of these faults. More than once, I nearly chose the easier way of storing the whole batch of papers and notes alongside a score of similar files on my shelves still awaiting the revisions they are not likely ever to get. Revising lectures is a tricky business. If you leave them in anything like their spoken form, there is the continued risk of foreshortened argument. If you armor-plate them against professional criticism, they become something else again.

But there were three considerations on the other side that finally outweighed my better judgment. The first was the stipulation in the invitation that the lectures be published. Thus, the assignment was itself a commitment. That, however, was not decisive; academic folk understand very well that such "conditions" are better left discretionary. But, then, there was the supporting fact that a sizable number of the people who had heard the lectures or who read the manuscript—and whose critical judgment I trust more than my own in a case like this—have urged that these particular lectures might be worth a wider audience. And, finally, there was my own imprudent impulse to stand up and be counted, at this particular juncture, in a public confession of personal faith in the God and Father of our Lord Jesus Christ. This, I know, is a flouting of the temper of the times, dominated as they are by the principle of theological displacement—and I do not do so bravely. Moreover, it goes against my grain to appear, even by implication, as a defender of the standing order, in the church and modern society.

But I've been convinced a long while now that much of the eager dismantling of "traditional beliefs" in our time has been possible largely because of widespread ignorance or misunderstanding of what those traditions really amount to in their basic intent and spirit. At the same time, I am altogether unconvinced that any of the radical alternatives thus far proposed holds any serious promise for the future of belief. My highest hope, therefore, would be to have at least a few others come to share my belief that the Christian tradition is far from being exhausted even in "modern" times, and that the Augustinian formula (*credo ut intellegam*—"belief is the precondition of understanding") is still the way to wisdom.

Another hope I have is that it also might occur to some that the *ad hominem* claim of the radicals to a copyright on "modernity" admits of honest doubt. One of the tests of truth is its viability in circumstances radically altered from its original matrix. Hence the question as to whether "traditional beliefs" are still viable must involve constant experiment in reassessing their intent and reformulating their essential meanings in *successive* "modern" contexts—"modern" always understood as a transient condition with its own built-in obsolescence. After all, what was "modern" yesterday is often already outdated "today," as every preacher knows who is still stuck with what he learned in seminary! It has been my life-long vocation to be as faithful as I could to the perduring truths of the tradition and as alert as I was able to the "modern" settings in which they could be reformulated as contemporary insights. And even if I have not realized my goal, its validity has never seemed doubtful.

The choice of the title was arbitrary. It is, of course, the first line of Joachim of Magdeburg's *Wer Gott vertraut, hat wohl gebaut*, which has often served me well as a rallying-cry in times of faltering faith and courage. But for its use as a peroration (pp. 134–35) the more literal and awkward translation by Catherine Winkworth was clearly more adequate.

The choice of a sub-title, however, was meant to be significant—and to anticipate the only criticism of this book I would wish to forestall in advance. These *are* musings; and musings are as much as I can manage in the flux and ferment of these days. The time for definitive systematic essays may come again before this century is out, but it is not now. And I am neither so compulsive nor so gallant as to waste insufficient talent on an untimely attempt at summing up a disorderly debate still in full cry.

My debts here, as elsewhere, are more than my assets and most of them will have to go unlisted. But I must begin my explicit acknowledgments with a word of loving tribute to Dr. James A. Jones who, as president of Union

Theological Seminary, issued the invitation to do these lectures but who died in the autumn (November 17, 1966) before the spring in which they were delivered. He rests from his labors, but the fruits of his labors for theological education will remain as a perpetual memorial, both at Union Theological Seminary and elsewhere. Acting President Balmer H. Kelly was my gracious host and sponsor during my visit to Richmond and my memories of those days are happy and grateful. I owe special thanks to Professor John H. Leith of the UTS faculty, once a student of mine and now an esteemed colleague in the field of historical theology. His firm but critical support of this and other projects has been invaluable. There were also other members of the faculty who were helpful over and beyond the call of duty: Professors James H. Smylie, John Thomas, Ross MacKenzie, and Henry M. Brimm. And the students, God bless them, who kept coming to lecture after lecture and who wanted to talk about them in between—I owe them more than a word here can convey.

In the revision of the lectures I have had the generous encouragement of my colleagues, Dean Joseph D. Quillian, Jr., and Professor James A. White—plus the careful criticism of Mrs. Keith M. Johansen, a highly competent "sample" of those literate "modern" layfolk whom I would greatly cherish as readers. But most of all, and for the whole of this project, I am indebted to and grateful for the expertise and faithfulness of Mrs. Wanda W. Smith, a jewel of a secretary.

Dallas, Texas A. C. O.
Labor Day, 1967

Acknowledgments

It is a pleasure here gratefully to acknowledge permission from the following publishers to quote cited passages from books on which they hold copyright:

Abingdon Press: *God's Way with Man; Variations on the Theme of Providence*, Roger Hazelton.

George Allen & Unwin, Ltd.: *Reformed Dogmatics*, Heinrich Heppe.

The Bobbs-Merrill Company, Inc.: *Radical Theology and the Death of God*, Thomas J. J. Altizer and William Hamilton, copyright 1966 by Thomas J. J. Altizer and William Hamilton.

George Braziller, Inc.: *The Tower and the Abyss: An Inquiry into the Transformation of the Individual*, Erich Kahler.

Sigmund Freud Copyrights, Ltd., Mrs. A. S. Strachey and Hogarth Press, Ltd.: *Civilization and Its Discontents* (1930), Vol. 21, The Standard Edition of the Complete Psychological Works of Sigmund Freud, and W. W. Norton & Company, Inc., American publishers and copyright holders of Sigmund Freud, *Civilization and Its Discontents*, translated by Joan Riviere.

Harper & Row: *The Essence of Christianity*, Ludwig Feuerbach, translated by George Eliot. *Interpretation: A Journal of Bible and Theology:* "The Question of God," Wolfhart Pannenberg.

Alfred A. Knopf, Inc.: *Joseph the Provider,* Thomas Mann, and *The Enlightenment: An Interpretation,* Vol. I, *The Rise of Modern Paganism,* Peter Gay.

Macmillan & Co., Ltd.: *Evil and the God of Love,* John Hick.

The Macmillan Company: *Letters and Papers from Prison,* Dietrich Bonhoeffer, and *The Historian and the Believer,* Van A. Harvey.

Open Court Publishing Company, La Salle, Illinois: *Religion Within the Bounds of Unaided Reason,* Immanuel Kant, translated by Theodore M. Greene and Hoyt H. Hudson.

Charles Scribner's Sons: *Jesus Christ and Mythology,* Rudolf Bultmann, and *Chance and Providence; God's Action in a World Governed by Scientific Law,* William G. Pollard.

The Society for Promoting Christian Knowledge: *Divine Providence and Human Destiny,* L. E. Elliott-Binns.

SCM Press and Westminster Press: *Augustine: Confessions and Enchiridion,* Library of Christian Classics, Vol. VII.

University of Chicago Press: *Systematic Theology,* Vol. III, Paul Tillich, copyright 1963.

Westminster Press: *The Gospel of Christian Atheism,* Thomas J. J. Altizer, copyright 1966, W. L. Jenkins.

Contents

I The Good Conscience of Modern Disbelief, 3

II Nature, History, and Grace, 31

III Providence as Presence, 57

IV God's Providence and Man's Anguish, 83

V Providence and the Christian Style of Life, 111

Index, 137

Who Trusts in God

I

The Good Conscience of Modern Disbelief

Christianity has had an endless series of crises to survive, and each has seemed to some the end of the line. The crises have come in manifold forms and with varied effects. There have been internal disruptions (schisms, doctrinal disputes, corruption and decadence, struggles for reform and renewal, etc.). There have been external pressures (persecutions, ideological mutations, the perennial tensions between Christianity and culture, etc.). And now we have one on our hands that is a curious compound of almost all that went before. The Christian community is still in crippling schism, despite a half-century of heroic and massive ecumenical efforts. The theological forum is a bedlam. The advocates of reform and renewal are numerous and clamant—but so far ineffective. In many parts of the world, Christianity is actively persecuted or suppressed (there have been more Christian martyrs in this century than in any other). Elsewhere, Christianity is all too comfortably domesticated in societies it does not deeply affect. But the most distinctive and significant feature of our particular time of troubles is the massive change in the ideological climate in "Western civilization" and its spin-offs, and the demoralizing impact of this on popular Christianity—clerical and lay. The most familiar slogan for identifying this change is Bonhoeffer's phrase about the world "come-of-age"; its most frequent allegement is that historic Christianity is no longer relevant to "modern" man's self-understanding—"modern" man being defined as one to whose self-understanding historic Christianity is no longer relevant!

Such things, of course, have been said before. Disbelief and displacement are typical reactions in every crisis. But in this current situation we have a unique configuration of forces. In the long history of doctrinal conflict in the Christian community, the central question has been the truth and meaning of Jesus Christ as God's revealed wisdom, power and love—the reality of God and his relevance to the human enterprise being allowed by all parties in the Christological disputes. Thus the theological task centered on the ideas of the Trinity, "the two natures," the history of salvation, the Christian ethic—and all of these in relation to the question of definitive authority (Scripture, tradition, etc.). In each of the major controversies anthropology has been an important side-issue. In the long history of Christian philosophy the cardinal topic has been the warrant for the truth-claims of Christians in respect of their knowledge of God and of his unity and sovereignty. Here the gamut has been run between the extremes of dualism and pantheism. But in Christian philosophy, as in theology, anthropology has been typically derivative. In both cases the ordinary forms of disbelief were "heresy" (the rejection of the doctrinal implicates of faith) or "atheism" (the rejection of the possibility of faith itself).

"Heresy" and "atheism" are still with us—without the churches and within! But what is different and very nearly unprecedented is a new modality of disbelief which is less interested in refuting Christian doctrine than in bypassing the whole business in the name of a Christian humanism that professes to sublate all the significant values in the tradition into one or another version of "religionless Christianity," "secular Christianity," "the new essence of Christianity," "*Christian* atheism," or what have you. In the good old days of "the warfare between science and theology," a self-respecting disbeliever would never use the word "God" as an affirmative indicator. Nowadays, there is an embargo on "God-talk," but only in the contexts of traditional theology. It is, in fact, fashionable within the new anthropological frames of reference that have come to dominate current theology. Even in the ruckus about "the death of God" it turned out that what was really at stake was not so much the death of *God* as the burial of the *deus et machina*—a job that some of us thought had been attended to a century and a half ago. But this interment was only incidental to a higher goal: the affirmation of man's maturity. It is interesting to see a "death of God" mortician like William Hamilton gently disengage his own position from "ordinary Feuerbachian atheism" in order to argue for a radical humanism that still comes very close to the original program of the entire Hegelian "left-wing." [1]

1. Thomas J. J. Altizer and William Hamilton, *Radical Theology and the Death of God* (Indianapolis: The Bobbs-Merrill Company, Inc., 1966), p. 41.

The lasting significance of this hurrah about "radical theology" and the "death of God" is its revelation of the spread and penetration of disbelief—in the churches as well as in the "modern" world—in the *deus ex machina*, the Man Upstairs, the executive deity of "I Believe." One might regard this form of disbelief as healthy—disbelief in the little god who wasn't there—except for the fact that it has all too often swept out the whole idea of God, as if the *deus ex machina* and the God and Father of our Lord Jesus Christ were and always had been identical. Time was when disbelief took itself outside the Christian community—when it was marginal and defensive. Now, in its modern humanist mutations, it is rampant and aggressive in the churches with a good conscience because it is less concerned with conventional denials (à la Ingersoll) than with its ringing announcement that the Kingdom of Man is "at hand," here and now, in the secular city. The *civitas terrena* has been baptized and canonized—repent and believe *this* good news! The world "come-of-age" means man on his own in a cosmos that has no room and no need for God. And with this triumphant revelation, out goes the linchpin of traditional Christian doctrine: the belief in the providence of God as the ultimate environment of human existence. This is the crux of our crisis, and its scope and purport are as grave as any our forefathers ever had to face.

For those of us who believe that historic Christianity will survive this crisis, and even be enriched by it—by the grace of that same providence that has sustained her hitherto—the way forward does not begin in outrage and counterattack but in renewed perspective and new efforts at reformulation. We need, first of all, to remind ourselves of how we got to this point in time and mind. Then we need to understand the issues involved, in the terms of those who have helped define them. And, finally, we must address these issues as calmly and positively as we can with what we take to be the perennial truth of the Christian message, in its "modern" context. Such an undertaking may very well bring snorts from the hot gospellers of humanism, nor should one hope for thanks from the museum guards of fossil-Christianity. But the essential task of the Christian apologist is not to search out and destroy the enemies of Christian truth, nor to coddle it from shocks and bruises, but to bear witness to his own understanding of the Gospel with whatever clarity and integrity he can muster. If it is God's truth, it cannot be finally nullified. If we are deluded, we can at least be honest.

The place where I would suggest beginning is with what Peter Gay has correctly identified as "the rise of modern paganism." [2] It began in the eighteenth century, with Voltaire for its first great prophet. He, more than any other, turned the genteel negations of deism into a furious onslaught against Christianity as such. "Every sensible man, every honorable man," he declaimed, "must hold the Christian sect in horror." [3] His battle cry, *Ecrasez l'infâme*, did not limit itself to the reformable faults of conventional Christianity (Roman Catholic or otherwise) but to Christianity, root and branch [4]—and his justification for his hostility to Christianity was his love for humanity.

2. *The Enlightenment: An Interpretation* (New York: Alfred A. Knopf, 1966), Vol. 1: *The Rise of Modern Paganism.*

3. *Oeuvres*, XXVI, 298.

4. Cf. Gay, *op. cit.*, pp. 389–92.

The Christian God, he thought, was hideously cruel and must be repudiated by men who want to be free to love their fellow men. *Je ne suis pas Chrétien, mais c'est pour t'aimer mieux* ["I am not a Christian, but it is in the interest of being able to love better"].[5]

This judgment that Christianity had to be abandoned for man's sake was urged more calmly by David Hume (of whom John Wesley observed that he had "found out both a religion and a happiness which have no relation at all to God, nor any dependence upon him" [Sermon CXIV, sec. 19]).

> Hume was willing to live with uncertainty, with no supernatural justifications, no complete explanations, no promise of permanent stability, with guides of merely probable validity; and what is more, he lived in his world without complaining, a cheerful Stoic. Hume, therefore, more decisively than many of his brethren in the Enlightenment, stands at the threshold of modernity and exhibits its risks and its possibilities. Without melodrama but with the sober eloquence one would expect from an accomplished classicist, Hume makes plain that since God is silent, man is his own master: he must live in a disenchanted world, submit everything to criticism, and make his own way.[6]

But Hume died in 1776, Voltaire in 1778. Their works have beeen staple reading for cultivated men for two centuries. What requires accounting for is the fact that their "modern disbelief" has only just now become epidemic, after such a time-lag.

There are at least three explanatory factors worth

5. *Épitre à Uranie*, quoted in Gay, *op. cit.*, p. 387.
6. Gay, *op. cit.*, pp. 418–19.

citing. The first is that, despite the unchecked and irresistible progress of science and technology for three centuries, it is only in our own century (actually, within our own generation!) that the basic ideas and the practical possibilities of the scientific enterprise have come to be shared universally—everywhere and by everybody. In this sense, "modern" means the conviction that what man can make can make life good for man. We shall have a later occasion to doubt that this secular eschatology is finally credible, but there is no denying its widespread acceptance today by literate and semi-literate alike. It is the moral nerve of modern technology and its propaganda.

A second stimulus in this recent spread of humanistic piety is what is spoken of nowadays as "the rise of historical consciousness," with its distinctive meaning for modern man's self-understanding. My colleague, Professor Van Harvey, has probed this problem in an important new book, *The Historian and the Believer*. "The heart of the issue before us is the collision of two moralities of knowledge, the one characteristic of the scholarly world since the Enlightenment, the other characteristic of traditional Christian belief." [7] The pathos of the modern mind arises from the conflict between man's *need* to believe more than he ever can know and his distrust of any belief that goes beyond the evidence (whatever that is):

> This pathos is intelligible only if we realize that the revolution in consciousness, which came about with the emergence of historical thinking, is fundamentally a revolution in the morality of knowledge. A new ideal of judgment has gripped the intellect of

7. Van A. Harvey, *The Historian and the Believer* (New York: The Macmillan Company, 1966), p. 127.

> Western man, and the student sensed that this ideal is incompatible with the ethic of belief that has so long been implicit in Christendom. The old morality celebrated faith and belief as virtues and regarded doubt as sin. The new morality celebrates methodological skepticism and is distrustful of passion in matters of inquiry. If Pascal's belief that the heart has its reasons which the reason cannot know can be said to represent the old ethic, then Nietzsche's conviction that integrity in matters of the mind requires that one be severe against one's heart may be regarded as symbolic of the new one. The old morality was fond of the slogan "faith seeking understanding"; the new morality believes that every yes and no must be a matter of conscience.[8]

And to an increasing number of men who have come to assume that science supports the notion that man is on his own in a "a closed universe," the faith of religious humanism seems as far as their consciences will let them go.

A third, and rather different, factor in the crisis is the domestication of religious humanism *within the churches*, either as a redefinition of traditional Christianity or as its displacement. The impact of the Enlightenment on Protestantism was vast and radical, but for the better part of two centuries it was absorbed into the basic framework of historic theism. The great architects of "liberal theology" (Schleiermacher, Ritschl, Bushnell) made drastic revisions in their reformulations of traditional doctrine but never dreamed of undercutting its foundation. Schleiermacher defined the very essence of religion as "absolute dependence"—the exact antithesis of humanism's first premise. Ritschl and Bushnell had powerful convictions about

8. *Ibid.*, p. 103.

God's creative and redemptive love as the primal source and energy of man's existence and well-being.

In the long struggle between "fundamentalism" and "modernism" (to settle for labels in lieu of analysis) the issues did indeed focus on the nature of *Christian* humanism—witness the affinities between "liberalism" and "the Social Gospel"—but they never struck at the root of the matter and they never came close to reducing theology to anthropology (although the fundamentalists regularly charged that this is what the modernists were up to).

Actually, this anthropological reduction had already taken place alongside and outside the Christian churches—there is a continuous tradition of it that runs from Immanuel Kant to John Dewey. Kant's interest in religion—apart from his destructive analysis of "ecclesiastical faith"—was earnestly moral.

> The theoretical part of ecclesiastical faith cannot interest us morally if it does not conduce to the performance of all human duties as divine commands (that which constitutes the essence of all religion).[9]
>
> Without either renouncing the service of ecclesiastical faith or attacking it, one can recognize its useful influence as a vehicle and at the same time deny to it, *taken as the illusory duty of divine worship*, any influence upon the concept of genuine (that is, moral) religion.[10]

Then there was Fichte's proposal that the good essence of Christianity was its perception of the divine in the human

9. Immanuel Kant, *Religion Within the Bounds of Unaided Reason*, translated with an Introduction and Notes by Theodore M. Greene and Hoyt H. Hudson (Chicago: The Open Court Publishing Company, 1934), p. 100.
10. *Ibid.*, p. 113. Italics added.

ego and Schelling's proposed displacement of the idea of God with that of the "absolute ego" or "absolute spirit." And all these led, though not by intention, to Feuerbach's triumphant climax:

> Faith in God is faith in the truth and infinity of human feeling. . . . Faith in the future life is . . . faith in the eternity and infinitude of personality . . . ; consequently, it is *the faith of man in himself*. . . . God is pure absolute subjectivity released from all natural limits; he is what individuals ought to be and will be: faith in God is therefore the faith of man in the infinite and truth of his own nature; the Divine Being is the subjective human being in his absolute freedom and unlimitedness.
>
> Our most essential task is now fulfilled. We have *reduced* the supermundane, supernatural, and superhuman nature of God to the elements of human nature as its fundamental elements. Our process of analysis has brought us again to the position with which we set out. The beginning, middle and end of religion is MAN.[11]

From Strauss and Baur to Harnack and Dewey the notion of human values as the immanence of the divine in man and history developed with a rich variety of themes and modulation on the fringes of popular Christianity. It was, in its way, a transfer of the old idea of the coinherence of "the two natures." The referent of the word God is the divine dimensions of human selfhood. The ethical significance of the phrase "communion with God" amounts to man's awareness of his full responsibility for

11. Ludwig Feuerbach, *The Essence of Christianity*, translated by George Eliot (New York: Harper & Brothers, 1957), p. 184. Italics added.

his own affairs—and this is "the essence of Christianity." This was a sort of secondary narcissism, with a built-in safety-hatch: if belief in God ever had to be abandoned, man would still be left with his human concerns suffused with religious feeling (Dewey).

Meanwhile, the Christian community seemed relatively steady and sound in its basic commitments to the historic foundation: God the provident creator and redeemer and man the dependent creature. In England, religious humanism made small headway within the confines of the Anglican Establishment until quite recently; I can remember when odd-angled characters like Bishop Barnes of Birmingham were walled off as nuisances. In America, the bid by the Unitarians to emancipate Christianity from its overburden of supernaturalism was easily contained, even by a Protestantism already moribund in New England. "Modernism" made no inroads at all in American Catholicism until the shock waves of Vatican II began to strike home.

Thus, liberalism in mainstream Protestantism stayed well within the bounds of traditional theonomy. It produced new theses about man's responsibility for his own history and worldly well-being. It stripped classical Protestantism of its last vestiges of infallibility (biblicism, etc.). The critical dissection of the Bible was carried forward—ruthlessly and to the horror of the fundamentalists—by men who were professed historians but who plainly set more store by the ultimate significance of the canonical texts than other historians do by *their* documents. Even so, the corporate life of the churches continued vigorous with many new frontiers in evangelism, missions, Christian education, and "the social Gospel." It is worth remembering that

Latourette's "Great Century" was also the "Liberal Century."

What then happened, as those of you past fifty can testify, was that the continued evolution of liberal Christianity (wherever it was headed) was diverted by a major theological revolution that proceeded to dominate the Protestant forum from the 'twenties to the 'sixties. This was a convergence of a variety of dynamic theological projects, all having as their common character some sort of synthesis of sixteenth- and nineteenth-century motifs—i.e. blends of classical *and* Enlightenment Protestantism. These blends picked up the omnibus designation, "neo-orthodoxy," not because they were homogeneous—far from it! —but because they shared two tendencies that were common to the old orthodoxy and opposed to the spirit of the Enlightenment. On the one hand, neo-orthodoxy withdrew the root issues of faith from logical analysis and metaphysical judgment. This was a renewal of the Reformation's rejection of "natural religion" in general and of analytic reason in particular. Salvation is by faith. Faith is God's gift—in Barth's famous phrase, *Senkrecht von oben* ("straight down from above"). In revelation, the divine initiative is absolute. Man's appropriate response in faith is not religion (Barth is fairly savage about "religion" in *Church Dogmatics* I/2!) and not assent to communicable truth, but radical trust in God's revealed and unmerited mercy—"existential faith," as they taught us to say. All the neo-orthodox titans (Barth, Brunner, the brothers Niebuhr, *et al.*) reaffirmed the prime place of Scripture in theological reflection and all of them stressed one or another type of spiritualized ecclesiology—the church as "event," not to be identified with the all too obvious flaws in the all too visible ecclesiastical institutions.

Their second common tendency was the rejection of the notion of *homo religiosus* in any of its versions—man with innate capacities for the divine indwelling, man with "religious experience" in response to revelation, man called to participate in the divine perfections. Their aim here was the rejection of what they took to be man's sinful disposition to corrupt his natural knowledge of God into idolatry (Calvin). Thus they dismissed exemplarism out of hand and reacted against any suggestion of synergism. They talked about the *kerygma* (their version of "the essence of Christianity") and *eschatology* (their substitute for the now tainted term, "supernatural").

But to all these Reformation (and pietist) motifs were added themes and accents that sharply differentiated neo-orthodoxy from any of the surviving forms of eighteenth-century Protestant *orthodoxy*—and this was quickly noticed by the "orthodox." *Neo*-orthodoxy shared much of the reductionist temper of liberalism—and many of its political, cultural and social ideas as well. It was as if the successive revolutions of Kant, Marx, and Freud were grafted onto the Reformation stock of Calvin and Luther. In this sense, the neo-orthodox were truly "modern," for their day. They sought to defend the faith once for all delivered, but some of their weapons would presently be turned against them.

And so it happened. The episode of neo-orthodoxy has closed with startling abruptness. Its geniuses are dead or retired, with no successor of comparable stature or promise. The upcoming generation has adopted a different style in their theologizing—invariably with the accent on God's making *the human scene!* One feels his age (and the *sic transit gloria mundi* bit) when present-day seminarians report their readings in Barth and Tillich in the same retrospective mood they bring to Ritschl and Schleiermacher —and Luke-Acts!

There was, as we knew, as vigorous a strain of skepticism in neo-orthodoxy as in liberalism. I well remember the tremendous impact of Søren Kierkegaard, who taught us that truth was subjectivity—and so strengthened the case against rationalism and for narcissism. There was Heidegger's demolition of the *philosophia perennis* (though many more people believed the *report* that he had done so than verified it!)—and with it there came a sort of final consensus that Christian metaphysics was an exercise in futility. We were taught to hail the Gospel echoes in Sartre's clarion calls to human freedom—without being bothered by Sartre's own personal experiments in freedom or the anti-humanistic ending of *Huit Clos.* What we were after, and what we believed we could achieve, was a Christianity from which all that could be shaken had been, so that what could not be shaken would remain. This would be "true Christianity," freed from its burdens of overbelief, cleared of the suspicion of incredulity. Surely the world would take such a faith seriously—or at the very least, we could live in it with a good conscience before God and without offense to our secular neighbors.

It was a sad case of over-confidence. What we had failed to reckon with was the almost sudden confluence of a number of basic changes that amounted to a revolution, with consequences that we are just now recognizing.

There was the swiftly spreading sophistication (and pseudo-sophistication) of the citizenry of our cities—most of them graduates of secular colleges or church-related colleges no less secular in actual orientation. Here was a major fraction of the only class not yet alienated from the churches, newly indoctrinated with various popular versions of the philosophy of science and at least the premises of modern sociology and psychology. Again, there was the swift collapse of "customary morality" and the broad-scale triumph of ethical relativism. We have now the first generation in Western history with vestigial super-egos! The consequence has been a massive shift of the ethical center of gravity from "society" (heteronomy) to the individual (autonomy), from universal rules to contextual decisions. Then, there was the emergence of powerful lay movements in the churches, deeply concerned to participate in the life and work of the churches, with but scant acquaintance with their Christian heritage. This was due to the near-total failure of the churches in transmitting the Christian tradition as a live option to modern men. Further, there is the mass exodus from the countryside to the spreading cities that is emptying the country churches, long the main reservoirs of conventional orthodoxy. Finally, there has been the passing of the "parson." Once upon a time, the minister or priest was the paragon of Christian culture in his congregation and often in the whole community—"the *parson* of the town." As such, it was the badge of his superior education to be more critical of traditional ideas than the less literate faithful—always, of course, in the interest of a valid faith tested by that snatch from Tennyson about "more faith in honest doubt . . . than in half the creeds." Nowadays, however, the minister is rarely the best-educated man even in his own congregation and, what is worse, his own first-hand acquaintance with the Christian heritage is rarely broad and deep. Taken all together, these developments have drastically altered the climate of belief within the churches themselves and the image of the churches in modern society.

The sin for which we may not be forgiven (since we are so far unrepentant of it!) is that, in such a time and amidst all the heroic struggles to make the Christian message relevant to a world in convulsion, we have despised, as indoctrination, the task of grounding the people in our churches in the substance of historic Christianity. It could scarcely be more ironic that just when we have come to be so clear and emphatic about the urgency of the Church's "witness" in and to the world, more and more Christians know less and less about the historic content of that "witness." When someone says that traditional Christianity has had it, there is hearty assent (and book buying!) by people with only the foggiest notion of what it is they are "discarding." And so they are more and more inclined to the thesis that, in the beginning, man created God to serve the human cause.

Perhaps it was inevitable, sooner or later, that the conflation of theology and anthropology would turn up in the churches as the newest "essence of Christianity." And it was not at all unnatural that it should have happened in Germany, in response to the hideous pressures of the Nazi nightmare. It is important to remember that Bultmann's original program for demythologizing the Bible was a response to the charge by the "German (Nazi) Christians" that the Evangelicals were hypocrites and frauds, preaching from texts about ascensions and angel-choruses which they could not possibly believe. Bultmann's reply admitted the very last part of the charge and denied the rest. Nobody anymore believes in a flat earth or in angels with vertical take-off and landing facilities. The biblical world-view, he suggested, was expressed in the form of *mythos*, and this world-view not only might, but should, be "demythologized"—which sometimes seems to mean "transvaluated," sometimes "discarded." Bultmann's definition of myth presupposed the new anthropocentrism. Myth, he said, is a form of language that attributes

> to the transcendent reality an immanent, this-worldly objectivity. Myths give worldly objectivity to that which is unworldly. (In German one would say, "Der Mythos objektiviert das Jenseitige zum Diesseitigen" ["myth makes what is past our knowing seem as if it were within our grasp"].) [12]

The proposal that such "objectifying language" should be purged is coupled with another dictum about the world as a closed system—and, together, they mark a turning point in modern theology. "Modern men [including Bultmann, of course] *take it for granted* that the course of nature and of history, like their own inner life and their practical life, is *nowhere* interrupted by the intervention of supernatural powers." [13]

Read one way, this is a healthy disbelief in the *deus ex machina* and in "God-talk" that pretends to any sort of

12. Rudolf Bultmann, *Jesus Christ and Mythology* (New York: Charles Scribner's Sons, 1958), p. 19.
13. *Ibid.*, p. 16. Italics added.

"God-handling." In its total context, however, it was readily understood as radical skepticism yoked with a radical anthropocentrism. Bultmann went on talking, with moving sincerity, about God as acting in the world and in human existence, about demythologizing as "the radical application of the doctrine of justification by faith to the sphere of knowledge and thought," [14] and repeating his assertion that the whole idea was paradoxical—as indeed it was! But what remained as an increasingly effective solvent of conventional belief was the double stress on non-intervention and on biblical faith as a mode of *self*-understanding.

It was Dietrich Bonhoeffer, in a Nazi prison, who put the paradox of human autonomy and Christian faith more and more starkly.

> God is being increasingly edged out of the world, now that it has come of age.[15]
>
> The only way to be honest is to recognize that we have to live in the world *etsi deus non daretur* ("as if God were not a given").[16]
>
> There is no longer any need for God as a working hypothesis, whether in morals, politics or science. Nor is there any need for such a God in religion or philosophy (Feuerbach). In the name of intellectual honesty these working hypotheses should be dropped or dispensed with as far as possible. A scientist or physician who seeks to provide edification is a hybrid.

14. *Ibid.*, p. 84.
15. Dietrich Bonhoeffer, *Letters and Papers from Prison* (New York: The Macmillan Company, 1966), p. 208.
16. *Ibid.*, p. 219.

> At this point nervous souls start asking what room is left for God now. . . .[17]

Bonhoeffer's answer to the "nervous souls" was a strange mixture of Lutheran pietism in support of his "modern" notion of autonomy:

> Our coming of age forces us to a true recognition of our situation *vis à vis* God. God is teaching us that we must live as men who can get along very well without him. The God who is with us is the God who forsakes us (Mark 15.34). The God who makes us live in this world without using him as a working hypothesis is the God before whom we are ever standing. Before God and with him we live without God.[18]

This residue of traditional faith became more unembarrassed as the prison days stretched on and on:

> [August 23, 1944]
>
> Please don't ever get anxious or worried about me, but don't forget to pray for me—I'm sure you don't! I am so sure of God's *guiding hand*, and I hope I shall never lose that certainty. You must never doubt that I am travelling my appointed road with gratitude and cheerfulness. My past life is replete with God's goodness, and *my sins are covered by the forgiving love of Christ crucified.* I am thankful for all those who have crossed my path, and all I wish is never to cause them sorrow, and that they, like me, will always be thankful for the forgiveness and mercy of God and sure of it.[19]

17. *Ibid.*, pp. 218–19.
18. *Ibid.*, p. 219.
19. *Ibid.*, p. 245. Italics added.

If this is "come-of-age," then so were Spener and Wesley!

What has happened in the years since Potsdam is that the vogue of autonomy has burgeoned and the storehouse of piety has been steadily depleted. Pietism's traditional alienation from ecclesiastical Christianity has now been reinforced by a newly conscientious rejection of "supernaturalism." The result has been a popular outcry against traditional doctrines in the high-hearted conviction that the cause of being truly human can best be served by rejecting the past. There was Bishop Robinson's unaccustomed effort to be honest to God and its attendant sensation. There are Bishop Pike's current exercises in tweeking conservative sensibilities, and the outcries that have followed. But the climacteric of the whole movement toward a radically anthropocentric faith came with the eruption of the "death of God" "theology"—a phenomenon that regularly puts me in mind of Deuteronomy 32:30!

It is clear, of course, that Hamilton and Altizer have enjoyed the sounds and sights of shattered icons and the spluttering outrage of the icon-tenders—but this was rather more their fun along the way. First and last, they were crusaders for a radical and unqualified autonomy for man. They are less interested in the death of God than in the triumph of man—over God's dead body, so to speak.

> . . . There is no way, ontological, cultural on psychological, to locate a part of the self or a part of human experience that needs God. There is no God-shaped blank within man. Man's heart may or may not be restless until it rests in God. It is not necessarily so. God is not in the realm of the necessary at all; he is not necessary being; he is not necessary to avoid despair or self-righteousness. He is one of the

possibles in a radically pluralistic spiritual and intellectual milieu.

This is just what man's coming of age is taken to mean. It is not true to say, with Luther, *entweder Gott oder Abgott* [either God or an idol]. It is not true to say, with Ingmar Bergman, "Without God, life is an outrageous terror." It is not true to say that there are certain areas, problems, dimensions to life today that can only be faced, solved, illumined, dealt with, by a religious perspective.

Religion is to be defined as the assumption in theology, preaching, apologetics, evangelism, counselling, that man needs God, and that there are certain things that God alone can do for him. I am denying that religion is necessary and saying that the movement from the church to the world that we have taken as definitive of Protestantism not only permits but requires this denial. To assert that we are men moving from cloister to world, church to world, to say that we are secular men, is to say that we do not ask God to do for us what the world is qualified to do. Really to travel along this road means that we trust the world, not God, to be our need fulfiller and problem solver, and God, if he is to be for us at all, must come in some other role.[20]

For Professor Altizer, it is less important that traditional Christianity is incredible than that it is the enemy of human freedom, dignity, and happiness.

Christianity, and Christianity alone, has reduced human existence to sin and guilt, confronting a broken humanity with a wholly other God who demands total submission to his numinous and judgmental power. Religion assumes its most repressive form in the Christian religious tradition, because only here—and

20. Altizer and Hamilton, *op. cit.*, p. 40.

> in its historical antecedent, The Book of Job—may one find a God of naked and absolutely sovereign power, a God who was evolved out of a reversal of the movement of the Spirit into flesh, and who now for the first time becomes abstract, alien, lifeless, and alone.[21]

Altizer's self-designated key is William Blake and the key to Blake is his hatred of the Christianity he knew as the spoliator of the humanity he loved. The Christian *God* was Blake's *Satan.*

There is more at stake in all this than the rivalry of theological systems or the clash of hermeneutical principles. Most of us are no longer bothered—some of us never were—by the archaisms and discrepancies to be found so abundantly in the Bible. The biblical picture of a three-tiered world, etc. is not a myth. It is an error—i.e. a pseudo-scientific hypothesis that has been disverified, dangerous only to the literalist believer, or disbeliever. The Scriptures need not be expurgated or discarded because of the errors in them. They only need to be decoded—and so taken seriously—by critical minds and open hearts.

What *is* at stake, however, with urgency and import, is the doctrine of God's real *presence* in *this* world as we know it, and the credibility of our alleged knowledge of this presence, if any. Wolfhart Pannenberg has identified this issue with uncomfortable clarity:

> Talk of the living God, the creator of the world, is threatening to become a hollow sound today, even on the lips of the Christian. The term "God" seems to be dispensable, if not even a hindrance, in under-

21. Thomas J. J. Altizer, *The Gospel of Christian Atheism* (Philadelphia: Westminster Press, 1966), p. 45.

standing the reality of the world in which we exist, determined as it is by science and technology. The daily life of every person, and of the Christian too, is conditioned by a life and thought without God. This lived atheism is today the obvious point of departure for all reflective thought. Even the mere question whether God exists and who he is stands in need of special justification today, if such a question is to lay any claim to being taken seriously by men in general. The question of God as the ultimate ground of all being had become so fundamentally problematic to philosophical thought in the last 150 years that a real sensation is caused when a modern philosopher attempts to revive the ancient theme of a philosophical doctrine of God.

. . .

Secular atheism, that is, life and thought without God, is the established premise on which the question of God is being debated today. This is true also of Christian thought, to the extent that it cannot simply remain aloof from the assumptions of its own epoch, but must always relate itself to them in some way, even though that take the form of contradiction.[22]

Taken by itself, the "death of God" was a relatively brief episode. Already its excitements have faded. But it was a landmark for our time because it exposed as nothing else had done before it the disorderly hodge-podge of belief, misbelief, and disbelief in the churches, the fading loyalties of many in mainstream Protestantism, and the haphazard fortunes of theological "publicity." We know now what we only surmised before: that disbelief in tradi-

22. *Interpretation; A Journal of Bible and Theology*, Vol. XXI, No. 3, July, 1967, pp. 289, 290.

tional Christianity is now epidemic not merely among the intelligentsia but the literate masses as well. Modern man has finally laid claim to the autonomy that the Enlightenment pagans promised him long ago.

It is obvious that this requires a decisive mutation in the traditional patterns of Christian teaching and apologetics. Failing a firm faith in God's reality and sovereign grace, questions about Christology are finally meaningless. It is true that all the radicals speak well of Jesus, but this is a remainder of their vestigial piety and will sooner or later lose its force. If one is helped by Van Buren's conclusion that "Jesus seems to have been a remarkably free man," what then of Socrates, St. Francis, and Gandhi (all also "remarkably free men")? Here the only way open to religious humanism leads to a pan-anthropon of moral heroes —which seems scarcely "modern" in this age of "non-heroes"! And with the undercutting of Christology goes the rest of the staple items in traditional "systematics" —save anthropology, of course.

What is left at issue, then, is the first article of Christian teaching—"one God, All-governing Father, Creator of heaven *and earth*, and of all things, *visible* and invisible" —and this is now a *new* problem once again after all these years. But within the conventional forms of that problem, it is not the question of "existence" that matters most but "presence." "Existence" is not the real crux. There are curious slips here and there in all the radicals that betray their haunted sense of the holy. At the opposite pole are the fideists, like Hermann Gollwitzer, who deny any and all possible *rational knowledge* of God and still contend for the possibility of faith (which would seem to imply reality). Professor Pannenberg, who is at least as scrupulous as the rest of his contemporaries about the sin of overbelief, can speak somewhat serenely of "man's dependence on a ground which supports him in the openness of his existence and transcends all objective reality" and of "the power which determines all reality" and call "it" God.[23]

Thus, the root issue in the modern "problem of God" is the credibility of God's active "presence" *in this world*—personal and gracious—in the continuance of creation, in the vicissitudes of history, as the divine love in which we live and move and have our being. But *this* question is only another way of asking about divine *providence*, since all the different notions of providence have been so many different ways of talking about God's presence in those particular slices of existence that have mattered most to men. They were, by the way, "secular" doctrines, too, for all of them assumed that the makings of man's salvation were in *this* world, or nowhere. The point of maximum impact in the collision between traditional Christianity and modern disbelief, therefore, is just here—where men consider the possibility of reaffirming some notion of God's providence as an integral value in man's true well-being. And if one is willing to risk his reputation in an experimental restatement of the case for traditional Christianity in the "modern" world, the problem of providence is a better place than most to "test the spirits" (cf. I John 4:1).

This, then, is the venture of these lectures: to re-present in ruminative fashion what I take to be the gist of the traditional affirmations of God's provident presence in cre-

23. *Ibid.*, pp. 306, 309.

ation and history—and to do this out of a conviction that in these traditional ideas there are rich resources of wisdom about our existence and destiny in this "modern" world even for those who take some pride in being modern. Rightly speaking, of course, this is a job for a genius, and I have no delusions of grandeur—nor any martyr complex that preens before derision or dead silence. But theological geniuses are currently in short supply and it falls to the rest of us to carry on with the tasks at hand with whatever competence and courage we are provided. This is what "vocation" means, at least in "traditional Christianity."

There are three assumptions in such a venture that should be acknowledged at the outset as a way of setting the tenor and intent of the discussion. The first is a strong suspicion that the case for modern disbelief is neither as "rational" nor as "humane" as its advocates take for granted. We will speak of it, therefore, as if it were still very much on trial, in terms of its own principles. Neither the scientific world-view which it invokes nor the cause of humanity to which it appeals requires the conclusions of humanism, nor do they deny the possibility of other interpretations of nature and history and human destiny in terms more consonant with the genius of the Christian tradition. I am not interested in defying the "modern" world; but by the same token, I am not at all convinced that its alleged consensus is as critical or as moral as it believes. Specifically, I react against its systematic abuse of the *ad hominem* style of argument (you don't want to be un-"modern," do you?).

My second assumption is that the Christian tradition

may be handled with the loyalty and freedom that belongs to critical historiography. It was the work of fallible men struggling to comprehend the rational implications of their worship of God and their awareness of his apophatic revelations. The Mystery to which they turned in faith, and on which they reflected with what mental constructs they had available, was then spoken of in language aimed at clarifying Christian experience and helping to reproduce it. Theology is neither a game nor a purely rational exercise. It is an agony for *insight*, insight that is supported and enriched by further reflection on further experience.

My third avowed bias is that the "old morality of knowledge" is not inherently immoral, even for a "modern" man. I still hold to the Anselmian formula (*fides quaerens intellectum*), partly because I have not yet discovered *any* significant inquiry (*quaestio*) into matters that lie close to the human heart that does not begin with a faith-commitment (*fides*) of one sort or another. The moral probity of such a method must be tested in each of its three terms. The "faith" (*fides*) must be recognizably close to the Christian *consensus fidelium*. This is a hermeneutical question. The "seeking" (*quaerens*) must be open and critical, guided by the rules of evidence, with an equal aversion to superstition *and* pathological doubt. The "sound reasons" (*intellecta*) must be nearly enough consistent with the patterns of "modern" thought so that those who reject them will have recognized them as live options and those who accept them will be convinced and not merely conned.

By the same token, there is a corresponding demand on the interested reader, if he is willing to go on from here. It is not enough to be present passively, to be convinced by dint of rhetoric or to be left unpersuaded if one's own lost chord is not struck full-fingered. There is no promise here of edification as a reward for casual attention. The issues here—and the larger questions entailed—involve us all and also the future of Christian belief. Neither belief nor disbelief any longer comes easily, or without passionate participation. If what is said here is insufficient, what would be more truly sufficient? If there are comments here that are incredible, what alternatives would be more truly credible? If anything here seems well said, is it because it resonates with a previous bias, or has it been a clue to valid insight? If traditional Christianity must really be abandoned, let it not be so nearly by default as it has been in the recent past. And, if there is any warrant better than wishful thinking for our living and dying trustfully in God's providence, let us make sure that such a faith contains a powerful prod to life in the world—life that seeks the truth in a love for the neighbor, that is "secular" because it is God's world and "sacral" because God calls all his children to be holy. In an enterprise like this, we must do better than parrot the faith of our fathers. We must find authentic ways of our own for praising God and confessing his grace to all.

II

Nature, History, and Grace

It was the sad fate of the *deus ex machina* to fall victim to automation. His job has been taken over by a newly self-confident modern man and *his* machines. Much of what once was regarded as "super-natural"—because unmanageable—has been brought under the actual or potential control of human technology, whose claims now stretch from the infinitesimal to the infinite. There are, of course, a few unsolved problems even yet; progress is notoriously non-symmetrical. There are also some theoretical loose-ends to be tidied up; our "answers" keep churning up further questions with no end in sight. Even so, "modern" man has come to feel that all these are *our* problems. The power and the glory for solving them lie with *us*, here in the Kingdom of Man. This, indeed, is what the bid for "radical autonomy" is all about. The world and existence may be ever so radically contingent, but man is the measure of all that is significantly human, the measurer of all that really matters in his existence. And so, as technology expanded, the god of the gaps had fewer and fewer gaps to fill—and "modern" men are disinclined to keep a redundant god on the premises.

This is the fate of any idea of God that confines him to gaps and vacancies or that puts him on special duty for jobs that can be taken over in the course of further human progress. When "natural" and "super-natural" are simply opposed to each other, any expansion of the "natural" means a corresponding contraction of the "super-natural." And this is what has been happening in the world "come-of-age." When "human" and "divine" have been rivals, man's achievement of competency naturally means God's superannuation. That there have been such disjunctive tendencies in traditional theology cannot be denied. One of the worst of them has been our preoccupation with soteriology, as if God's chief (sometimes sole) business in creation is with *our salvation.* This has meant the rejection of "general revelation" and "natural religion," the denial of any knowledge of God save only through "the eyes of faith," the narrowing of Christian concerns to "ultimate" issues. This fideism is a special subjectivist version of the god-of-the-gaps theology: all we need of God is what we admit we cannot manage on our own—our "salvation."

On the other hand, if there is one constant and relatively consistent theme throughout the Bible and the whole of patristic Christianity, it is that God's business with creation embraces it all—the world at every level, existence in every form. He is, first and forever, the Creator, "of heaven and earth and of *all* things, visible and invisible." Creation is his deliberate project and it is wholly dependent on his constant creativity: this is what the "creation from nothing" (*de nihilo*) means. Creation is an ongoing business, with possibilities and capacities for *partial* sufficiency built into the entire complex. The providence of God means, first of all, his pro-duction of such a capacitated enterprise and his pro-vision for its continuance—including the pro-vision that it might go rightly or awry. Moreover, such provisions involve the preservation and sustenance of the project as a whole, within the given limits of finite space, time, and order. In this perspective, there is no notion of God's "fitting into" this gap or that. Rather, it recognizes and acknowledges God's sovereign providence in his appropriate relations to *every* conceivable level and category of creation: nature, history, spirit, or whatever.

This was, indeed, one of the prime motives in the development of the doctrine of the Trinity, from its doxological beginnings in the New Testament and the early Christian liturgies, to its dogmatic formulations by the fourth-century theologians. It was when Marcion and the Gnostics argued that the physical creation ("nature") was no fit arena for God's real presence and, later, when Arius proclaimed the utter transcendence of God the Father, beyond all human access, that the "orthodox" Christians had to translate their liturgical symbols of One-in-Three into "metaphysics," in order to "explain" their aboriginal belief in the "*All*-governing Father" (*Pantokrator*)—with its corollary that his providence is all-inclusive.

It was Origen who first worked out the notion that, in the "joint-operations" of the Holy Trinity, the primary "jurisdiction" of *God the Father* was *nature* in its fullest extent ("*all* things, visible *and* invisible"). The principal domain of God the Son is a special segment of nature: the *human enterprise*. This left the Holy Spirit with a special assignment in the development of human selves in *true community*—which meant, for Origen, the Church in its true holiness. This was at least one way of recognizing that persons and groups are rooted in their common humanity and that humanity is, in turn, rooted in universal nature. Turned around, this trinitarian view of creation means that nature reaches its climax in humanity, that humanity flowers in personal and communal relations, and that all three "levels" (nature, humanity, and "spirit") depend on the constant creativity of God for their existence and the fulfillment of their given possibilities. The distinctive characteristic of nature is orderly process; the unique feature of history is its revelation of the interplay of human freedom; the primary "mark" of the "church" is that it is the special locus of the Holy Spirit (God at work amongst men as *agape* and *charisma*). This triadic order for God's essential "functions" had the merit, Origen thought, of corresponding to the three concentric circles in which human existence is located: creation (nature in its broadest scope), humanity (historical existence), and spirit (selfhood).

To say that man is a creature is to say that, as nature's child, the whole range of his human experience (from birth to death) is radically involved in his sub-human environment and radically dependent upon it. Our lives are bracketed by antecedents and consequences beyond our initiation and control, beyond any conceivable final domination. This holds even for the prospect when the molecular biologists learn how to manipulate our chromosomes and prolong our lives by synthetic cell-regeneration, for then the brackets would only be shoved back, not erased. All men share with whatever else there is—"inanimate" or "animate" or "spiritual"—in an inescapable finitude. The Greeks and the mystery cults knew this and found it unendurable. The biblical and patristic authors knew it and made it the positive premise of their faith that men live best (are "justified") when they affirm their creatureliness and rejoice in its God-given possibilities.

Man is nature's child but he is an offspring with a difference. He is a creature but a self-conscious creature with unique powers of observation, assessment and exploitation which he exercises in ways that are neither uniform nor orderly. He is given the world to dominate but his own self-control is tenuous. Man is a biological organism whose stimulus-response activities generate conditioned reflexes (habits, attitudes, etc.) and yet also *insights* and *ideas* that require communication and community. Man is future-oriented, but his encounter with the future is conditioned by memories from the past and by at least occasional glimpses, in the fleeting present, of the eternal. Man makes culture and history as no other animal does; he transcends the limits of experience by thought; his cruelty and compassion are both "un-natural" in their extremes; his capacities for dignity and for degradation are not matched elsewhere in nature. He is both a problem and a mystery to himself and others; his history is different in quality and consequence to the life-cycles of any of his animal cousins.

To say that man is a "spirit" does not modify his status as a creature, or as a biological organism, or as an artificer of culture and history. It does not imply that he is some kind of spook haunting an animal body. The psycho-physical unity of man is an assured consensus in modern psychology and in biblical anthropology as well. What it means to be a "spirit" is that man has an inner thrust toward significant community that is very different from the herding patterns of any other animal. Man as "spirit" is communicant and communicator in ways that animals and thinking machines and hominids do not duplicate even by analogy. And the least that this can mean is that the special badges of our humanity—personal identity, freedom, capacity for selfless love—are none of them "natural," in the sense of being mere functions of our bio-psychological constitution. There is a dimension of every human self that is, in this sense, "supernatural" (a dirty word, I know, but let us not be squeamish), a mysterious reality that reaches out beyond the boundaries of time, space and the causal order. Man as spirit (selfhood) is man in concourse with the Creator Spirit— and with his fellow human spirits. This is the source of our true humanity, the bolster of the truest sort of *humanism.*

When we say "natural," we normally mean process and *order*, and a determinate process and order, at that. All the theoretical formulations of science (hypotheses, field-theories, laws, etc.) that account for any aspect of "nature" are deterministic in form and intent. "Nature" is an enclosed system of causes, and those causal theories are best that provide the simplest possible generalizations of the widest range of data. A unified field-theory—a universal formula capable of subsuming all specific models and theorems—is the ultimate goal of pure science.

In nature so conceived there is no place for God as "a

working hypothesis" and no need for him—if "working hypothesis" means assigning God as the direct cause of discrete events. God is no *part* of nature nor is he the *sum* of all its parts. There is, of course, a long standing confusion between God as *a* motion, *a* cause, *an* existent, on the one hand, and, on the other, God as the Provider of all the potentialities of motion, causality, and existence. This confusion has produced composite ideas of God as arbitrary motion and episodic cause which have been as unhelpful in theology as in science. This was how we got the *deus ex machina*, the deity for special occasions! And Bonhoeffer was right in saying that vis-à-vis *this* god, we could do better on our own.

We may wonder, however, whether Kant and the Protestant fideists were right in supposing that their rejection of the idea of God as a "working hypothesis" really disposed of the traditional arguments for God's reality. Kant's critique demonstrated the inappropriateness of including God in any of "the categories of the [human] understanding." But this was never the crux of the "proofs," never the essential idea of God to which they pointed. Their main contention—and here they were furnishing "modern" *intellecta* (i.e. when "medieval" was modern) for what they took to be the biblical *fides*—was that, since all creation is finite, *all* finites (small and great, gross or refined) are set in a matrix that is encompassed by the Eternal Mystery. This Mystery is immanent in every finite process at the same time that it also transcends all finites. Here, then, is the provident ground of the entire creation, with all its primordial possibilities; here is the ambiance of all its events and occasions; here is the Good that assesses the meanings and values that are achieved or aborted in the enterprise.

"Nature," in this perspective, *is* a "closed system," in the sense that its integrity is not threatened "from beyond" by episodic intervention or disorder. Natural processes are intelligible in and of themselves; miracles add nothing by way of scientific explanation. By the same token, however, nature is not fully autonomous and not at all self-explanatory. Every natural event or occasion happens *in medias res*. Our attempts to analyze them are regressive or progressive within quite arbitrary limits (e.g., the photo-electric effect, the Planck "constant," the speed of light). Nor, in the whole round of nature is there a clue as to why there should be order and uniformity and not random eventfulness. There is no proof at all that the correspondence between theory and experiment is *merely* a function of our mental constructs. There is no accounting for the heuristic success of the "scientific" method, based as it is on uniformitarian assumptions that once were incredible and are still beyond proof. To say that the meanings and values that men believe they "find" in nature are merely human investments in nature is denied by the fact that science is perpetually self-correcting—and this it would not be if each theoretical revision meant a parallel mutation in the corporate mental processes of whatever sample of mankind that espoused it. To say that such questions are "meaningless" simply raises the question about how "meaninglessness" is measured—and by whom? —and why this or that brand of naturalism is more "meaningful" than this or that theory of divine transcendence. Any more in this direction pushes reflection past the limits of analytic solution—onto metaphysical grounds where intelligibility is the prime canon. Here the case for nihilism amounts to an aesthetic penchant for the absurd. The rival case for naturalism is more rational than nihilism in that it does wield a certain veto power against narcissism, on the one hand, and superstition on the other. Agnosticism is not a metaphysical position but a methodological policy of suspended judgment—but till when? Christian monotheism does not propose to displace all other accounts of existence; it claims, rather, that it can include their good essences. It holds that it is rationally conceivable and morally licit to think of *nature as given* (pro-vided!), as a configuration of finite processes, contingent and interdependent but neither self-contained nor self-explanatory. It regards it as at least theoretically admissable to think of nature as a sort of "parenthesis," the full meaning of which is supplied "from beyond" without negating the significance of what lies "inside." Here, one might think, is a useful parable: the meaning of the entire sentence is "present" in a parenthesis without "intervention." The givens *in* nature are given *to* nature—but whence the gift and who the Giver?

What *is* absent from "nature," anywhere, is freedom. This is only another way of saying that nature is fully and consistently determinate—in this sense, "a closed system." Natural processes are fully immersed in the causal order; a "natural" item, event or configuration of events is one that is explicable and/or predictable by causal analysis, *without remainder*. Christian apologists should know by now that the "blank spots" in scientific explanations are not the likeliest places to seek for God. The "uncertainty theorems" (Gödel, Heisenberg) do not make room for God nor were they meant to. But they do remind us, first, that nature is unfinished and still evolving; second, that human observation affects both the phenomena observed and the observers in ways that produce formally insoluble problems within formally determinate processes; and, thirdly, that there are, therefore, irreducible paralogisms within and at the limits of scientific inquiry. These conclusions—one might have thought them commonplace—suggest that nature is finite and contingent and our knowledge of nature is finite and contingent. A unified field-theory of all gravitational and electrical phenomena is theoretically possible, but the *ground* of any such possibility would still go unaccounted for, save by some regressive analysis that pushes the limits of finitude further and further back—but literally without end.

Is this line of argument another paraphrase of the traditional "arguments"? Of their intentions, yes. We have (with Anselm and Aquinas as authorities for doing so) denied God's "existence" as *a* motion, *a* cause, *a* being—in order to affirm his reality as Provident Mystery that is the ground of *all* motions, *all* causes, *all* beings and the entire "cosmos" in which they co-exist. After all, the real aim of the classical "arguments" was to force the analyst back to the most primitive elements of sensible and rational experience (motions, recognition of causes, the tilt of human choice by values and purposes, etc.) in order to nudge him toward the crisis of *existential choice* between two final alternatives: either an infinite regress or the Provident Mystery ("God") as "terminus" for *any* inquiry about existence and its ultimate environment. Any analysis of motion (the precondition of all experience) yields the conclusion that the phenomenon of motion is "given" (i.e. *provided*). The causal order and all the categories of the understanding (the apparatus for "mental constructs") are also "given." Existence is "given"—and it is whatever it is as *given*, and not as constructed by human consciousness.

But what is the referent for the term "given"? To say that nature is given by nature is something less than an overpowering insight. To say we do not *know* is quite allowable and commendably modest, but then it must stand as an actually *suspended judgment* and not become the smuggled premise for some positive thesis about the eternity of matter. There is no logic that can coerce a man's choice between the two final alternatives—infinite regress or Encompassing Mystery—but there is no avoiding the choice, either, if only by implication. This is part of what freedom means and why belief and doubt coinhere in the same man—even in the heartiest believer.

But regress and providence are not really equal options. The one commits a man to a heroic and endless project that must finally be ended arbitrarily—as when chess players recognize a stalemate and settle for a tie. The other has the advantages of a positive conclusion (the psychological meaning of *belief*) whose warrants are as firm as any alternative and do not violate any legitimate moral inhibition of belief. To show that some such belief in the reality of God as the ground of the givens is consonant with the essential stipulations of "modernity" is an urgent task of contemporary apologetics. Given "clearance" on this point, Christian thinkers could proceed with their renovations of *the religious intentions of classical theism* in terms that would seek to satisfy the current canons of philosophical clarity and concreteness. Any renewal in this direction will entail drastic mutations of many of the forms and conventions of classical theism—and of "classical" rationalism and skepticism, as well. One sees the first signs of what may be the future of "neo-classical theism" along this line (Lonergan, Hartshorne, Ogden, Cobb). For the time being, however, it is enough to suggest that the warrants for disbelief in God as Provident Mystery are by no means as decisive as has been claimed and their triumphant negations cannot be made to stick.

We have said that we are nature's children, but that is not *all* we are. We are her *human* children, which is to say that we share in the vital confusions of *history* as well as the dynamic orders of nature. Our generation is more fully conscious than our fathers were of how radically historical human existence really is. "History" and "human existence" are mutual implicates. Rocks and trees and animals have "histories," too—but these are unremembered pasts which cannot be rehearsed or re-assessed and thus they do not serve as resources for self-understanding and conscious policy. Only humans have histories that preform their identities and reform their futures. This is why the proper study of mankind is *history*, for here we come upon that one capacity that is missing in nature: freedom, the well-spring of human grandeur and misery.

History is the arena of man's freedom—the intersection of the natural and the distinctively human, where man is never more than partially free but also never wholly determinate. It is, therefore, a different level of existence and it raises our constant question in yet another context. Is it at all allowable to conceive of God's Provident Mystery as active in human history in appropriately different ways than his providence for nature, without an indecent exposure of overbelief? Obviously, the answer here turns on our understanding of history.

A helpful place to begin our inquiry is with the analogy between history and gossip. The essential point to gossip —good, bad, or nattering—is its fascination with *personal narration:* people telling each other stories about people. The fact that some of these "stories" are false and very few fully accurate helps focus the persistent question that haunts the self-critical historian: what sort of "truth" is personal narration aimed at? The ruling interest in gossip, good or bad, is the human condition in all its variety and possibilities. Thus, our accounts of human behavior and experience are all aimed, curiously or critically, at one absorbing concern: *human character.* We want to know what other humans do and feel as a way of adding to our own experience of being human. By the same token, history is also focused mainly on the human scene and, thus, its truly distinctive concern is with the experience of being human. In this respect, history is full partner with literature and the arts in its efforts to civilize the human barbarian and to illuminate existence with the light that falls from the perspectives of the human past.

History, then, is gossip raised to a higher power, refined by the tools and temper of critical analysis and interpretation. As such, its liveliest interest is in the human condition—but with a different approach to it than those appropriate to the physical or the social sciences. The good historian is devoutly critical, he is highly skilled in relevant scientific procedures for gathering and sifting his data, he knows the rules of evidence and he is allergic to the cocked eyebrows of his colleagues. At the same time, his distinctive "field of intelligible inquiry" is one or another slice of humanity-in-past-time and his chief purpose in comprehending a given field is to be able to re-present it in the form of a *plausible narrative.* What is more, his success in making his narrative plausible will turn on his grasp of the motives, intentions, and performance of his cast of *human characters* and his skill in re-presenting the dramas they acted out. Instead of propounding *causal explanations*, the historian has to account for human *decisions* and "accidents," for these are the stuff of the drama he is representing. These "accidents" may be "natural," they may be wildly coincidental, they may be rational or "absurd." But they all have to be weighed, assessed—and colored by the historian's biases—in order to produce a plausible story, based on public evidence, that is reasonably faithful to the human characters involved. The good historian will refrain from drawing "morals" as scrupulously as he will from announcing "historical laws"—but he can scarcely ignore the function and effect of the moral choices made by the characters in his drama. In this way the historian is like, and yet also unlike, the novelist or the playwright. A novel is a cast of characters in search of a believable set of circumstances; a historical narrative is a set of circumstances in search of a believable cast of characters.

It is the genius of good history to provide human insight into lives and times other than our own. Thus it links their past with our future—in somewhat the same way the psychotherapeutic rehearsal of one's own past re-opens the future by allowing for the *transvaluation* of what has hitherto been misleading because it was misunderstood. History can re-present a given slice of the human past so that the reader can see it once again ("alive") in its complex rootage in nature (determinate), its participation in freedom (partially indeterminate), and its relevance for the contemporary struggles for community (personal and interpersonal).

But the lure of causality is well-nigh irresistible. In every inquiry there is the hunger for the power of predictive knowledge and consequent control. None of us is quite dead to the hope that we might discover reliable laws for historical prediction—for this way would lie an escape from the uncertainties of our self-understanding and also some hope of gaining real mastery over our human future, comparable to our technological domination of nature. Thus we slide over the line from history to metahistory without noticing, from *narration* to "scientific explanation"—to value-judgments that mirror our own.

But the fact remains that there are no causal explanations of historical events even closely analogous to the explanatory models that work so well in the natural sciences. Historical interpretation is, in the nature of the case, radically uncertain in any of its general "conclusions." No historical thesis can ever be *fully* verified.[1]

This is apparent in at least three ways. In the first place there is a radical difference between experienced and reported action. And, when the report is of long-remembered action, the attrition of memory and the distortions

1. There is a fuller discussion of this "uncertainty principle" in my article, "Theodosius' Horse: Reflections on the Predicament of the Church Historian," *Church History*, Vol. XXXIV, No. 3, September, 1965, pp. 251–61.

of hindsight cannot fail to reshape our cognition of the original action so that either it cannot be recovered intact or else such a recovery cannot be *proved*. The past is explicable only as having been determined; but when a given past event was a "present moment," it was not then experienced as *pre*-determined. There is, therefore, the constant specter of the *post hoc, ergo propter hoc* fallacy haunting every causal explanation of every historical event ("this came after that; therefore, it was *caused* by that"). In the second place, all historical perspective is paradoxical. There is a necessary interval between any given event and its optimum retrospect. But in this interval there is also an inevitable entropy of evidence, together with various alterations of the conditions in which recollection and rehearsal take place. This is why no given event can be fully understood until all its consequences are known, but this runs us, literally, out of time. In the third place, as Tolstoy argued so eloquently in *War and Peace*, "history is the integration of infinitesimals and accidents." We speak of "accidents" to denote happenings for which there would have been no rational *prediction*. Many of these so-called "accidents" have been seized upon as landing strips for the *deus ex machina*, as well as for various notions of providence as super-natural intervention: storms, epidemics, fractious horses, Cleopatra's nose. There is, indeed, a familiar legal phrase, "acts of God," which reminds us of how hopelessly ambiguous the whole idea is. Here, however, was the place where the god of the gaps could get a turn on the world's stage, where otherwise he was written out of the script.

This business of identifying God's providence with historical accidents is, of course, no help at all for rational belief. There is, for example, the story of the death of Theodosius II (A.D. 450)—from injuries sustained from a fall from his horse—an unexpected event that was followed by an extraordinary chain of events that altered the subsequent course of church and empire. There is Gibbon's gloss on the story to the effect that the cause of Constantinople was saved "by the fortunate stumbling of a horse." The difficulty, however, is that whether we think of that accident as "fortunate," or "providential" or "natural," it really does not provide the ground for any timeless truth about the deaths of "bad emperors" or the survival of the church. We shall presently affirm that God is the Provider of all the possibilities and meanings in human history as well as all the forms and processes of nature, but not till we have denied his role as cosmic magician. The invocation of providence or fortune to account for the twists and turns of history invariably proves too much or too little. The "providence" that saved England from the Armada, for example, was plainly anti-Iberian.

What is being suggested here is that human history is the domain where human freedom surfaces, in ways that escape determinism and that mark off history from the fully determinate realms of nature. If this is true, it would follow that God's presence in history would be correlated in some special way with the given-ness of freedom (its pro-vidence) and with its uses and abuses. But is *this* believable?

The case for determinism is formidable—and it turns on the apparent fact that human acts, when analyzed in retrospect, are seen to have been the sum of their antecedent impulses. Or, in the case of anticipated future actions, it can safely be predicted that when they will have occurred (i.e. when they are past events), they can then be analyzed as resultants of all their antecedents—even if some of those antecedents were not known or knowable beforehand. Both the past and the future are, thus, determinate; neither is a locus of human freedom. Here lies the strength of all the *pre*-destinarian arguments. Here lies the rock on which eschatologies that depend mainly on the future regularly founder.

What is rarely noticed in such arguments, however, is that all the deterministic schemes ("closed systems") ignore *the present*, or else regard it as nothing more than the transit point of time's swift passage from what is not yet to what is no longer. And so it seems to most of us, since we are so fully conscious of the perceptual frames of clock-time in which the present goes unrecorded, even by the fastest stopwatch. But, if present time cannot be measured, can it rightly be said to exist? The question is utterly crucial, for on it turns the reality of human freedom—and, indeed, the reality of the human self—since the self in its freedom never appears even as "object" in clock-time or in linear space. Let us, then, propose this thesis: time present ("the present moment") is not an indeterminate "gap" between the determinate past and future. If it is real at all, it is radically different from times past and future. It is, in short, the locus where the human self (otherwise "absent") becomes "present" in its true mystery of freedom, identity, and power to love.[2]

The biblical tradition clearly distinguishes between

2. There is a somewhat ampler exposition of this notion of the self and its freedom in my *Psychotherapy and the Christian Message* (New York: Harper & Row, 1966), pp. 56–98.

clock-time (*chronos*) and life-time (*kairos*). *Kairos* is not linear time. It is the "moment" of climax or crisis; whatever comes after any such "moment" is existentially different from what has gone before. The revelations, insights, decisions, and conversions that alter existence in its depths come in moments of present time (*kairoi*), which thereafter slide imperceptibly into the past, leaving only their affects "behind" in the lives of the participants. Decisions are made by people in clock-time, but the subjective springs of responsible decisions (as contrasted with competent calculations!) are somewhere off the calendar. This is why a really momentous decision is never wholly predictable. The present moment of freedom is always an added factor in the convergence of antecedent motives on the point of action—and cannot be fully calculated in advance.

St. Augustine noticed this long ago in Book XI of his *Confessions*. Past time is known, he says, by memory (*memoria*) and future time awaited by foresight (*expectatio*). Between them, and categorically different from either, is present time, which is never more than glimpsed. But these glimpsed "moments" have their own unique reality (*distentiones*), and our intuition of them (Augustine calls it *contuitus*) is the trigger of those free insights, decisions, conversions that happen "in the fullness of time." These moments of freedom are instantaneous, although their consequences are then absorbed into the consequent flow of *chronos* from future to past. When there is no contuition, life simply passes through us, dominated by determinate forces (reflexes, habits, customs, etc.). Time present, therefore, is the only time in which we live in our own "beyond." It is "the time of our life," the time of freedom and of self-chosen change (what the New Testament calls *metanoia*, "repentance").

Freedom is not a constant quality in human behavior nor is it ever unlimited. It is always bracketed by the determinate processes within which it is meshed. We are not free to cancel or defy the causal order. Instead, we are given (pro-vided!) the power to transvaluate our pasts (to give our memories new meanings) and to reappraise our futures (to refresh our hopes with new insights and vision). Freedom is the power of self-identification, self-acceptance, self-correction, etc. We *are* free, upon occasion, to repent, to trust, to glimpse the real meaning of acceptance, to love.

Chronological time is invariable; it ticks away regardless. Life-time is variable—it races or drags as life's interests lift and lower. Contuition is the spontaneous experience that gathers up the variables of psychological time in a fleeting episode (*distentio*) of recognition and decision. Thereafter, its memories and consequences blend into the incessant flow of clock-time. But now, our relation to both the past beyond recall and the future beyond control is different; there is a new meaning that has been added to life's "feeling tone" and quality. Contuition is spontaneous—out of space and time and, therefore, out of the causal nexus. Here, between past and future, is the turning point of "history"—of an individual's life history or of the human infinitesimals that tip the scales of history in the large. Here is where the uniquely human happens, where spirit and Spirit meet.

"What's done can't be undone." Yes, of course, but its meaning and its import for the future may be altered by recalling its significant events, re-living and re-assessing them. This is our freedom toward the past—and the most important of all our motives for historical inquiry. "What is to be, will be." Yes, of course, but it is always possible for what "is to be" to be affected by a self-conscious present moment of freedom before it has come to be—and then that "moment" (*kairos*) may be seen as one of the antecedent factors that "determined" the event. This is why no human future is fully predictable—even though it may be fully explicable when it finally becomes fully past. This is why history is not a science of causal explanations.

But part of the mystery of human freedom is that we do not generate *kairoi* on order or schedule. Our freedom is not, in that sense, deliberate. It is "given" (pro-vided) as a power that is truly our own but always in vital communion with its ground and source. Freedom accepted and abused is the antithesis of freedom accepted and rightly used—and the distinction between use and abuse is grounded in values that transcend subjectivity. The will to freedom is the very essence of our humanity, but we are ill-served by freedom that is not itself obedient to the requirements of selfless love. This is why so many of the existentialists and "the flower people" have had their bids for freedom turn to ashes and why the high and mighty of the earth so often fail in their titanic self-assertions.

Freedom, then, is the gift of whatever it is that provides our human existence. It is less the power to intervene in causal process than it is the power to act in the presence of that Provident Mystery that encompasses our lives. And, insofar as human freedoms make human history a unique dimension of nature and process, history is itself a work of providence—again, in the sense of being the resultant of the exercise of capacities that are *given* as ingredient in the human condition.

Here, then, is the ground of our human self-transcendence, of our concurrent participation in the processes of nature and in the life of the Spirit. To say that man is "spirit" is to say that, as *personal subject*, he transcends the limits of space, time, and causality—that his spirit communes with the Holy Spirit in the depths of its self-transcendence and on the margins of the infinite. It is to say that God the Provider is present "in" human life and history, not as intervener in natural process but as the provider of our freedom and the conditions of its appropriate use. God is not a physical cause. He is, rather, that pure unbounded love that environs and redeems our impure bounded loves and thus provides both order and grace as the matrix of existence.

In order to recognize God's Provident Mystery in our lives and histories, it is only required that we ponder the mystery of selfhood—and recognize our selves as *gifts* bestowed upon ourselves, gifts replete with purposes and powers that make all the difference in what our lives are meant to mean. The Mystery that provides these gifts is wholly beyond our manipulation or merited claim and thus transcendent. But it is also as immanent as our own "hearts" (our "subject-selves")—which is the "place" where we become aware of the possibilities of life in the Spirit (the Mystery turned personal, in *us* and for *us*!).

All of this is to say that God the Provider is not present in nature or history as body or physical force—although he is the source of the provision of order and process and sustains them within "their appointed bounds." In this sense, Bultmann's interdiction on "intervention" is valid. What is odd, however, is the unwarranted inference that so many have drawn that if God is not present in the world as physical force, he is therefore "absent." This is a sort of theological materialism—neither biblical nor rational. It ignores the two modes of divine being and creative presence that the New Testament stresses most: "God is Spirit," "God is Love"—the Johannine witness to Christ's incarnation of both divine Spirit and boundless love.

The Christian tradition, in contrast to the animism in which all too many Christians have remained, has a vivid sense of the reality of the Holy Spirit's presence in human lives and communities that is neither spooky nor "interventive." There is the analogy of interpersonal relations, where an "I" is truly present in a "Thou" without "intervention." This is an affective presence, too, but no laws of cause-effect relations can be inferred from it. Christian mysticism has often teetered on the brink—and often slid over it!—of the bizarre and exotic, but at its best it bears testimony to the reality of communion with the living God in human life and history. To say that "God is Spirit" is to say that he is "personal." And this is to say that his unwearied concern is with persons in their aspirations and with their communities as the environments that were meant to support those aspirations. This means that God is in history and its eventuations, never as spook or thaumaturge, but as Provider of the possibilities and opportunities of the enterprise and as Pastor to those who seek his loving enablement in their concerns for others.

We have noticed the rising tide of passion in our time that mankind shall come into its own, into the full measure of all that goes with being human—freedom, love, community, etc. We know ourselves now as the agents of our own culture and our own secular well-being. At this level, there is no Santa Claus, no cosmic Red Cross. But we've been at this experiment of "going it alone" long enough now to begin to suspect that there is something tragically wrong with the prescription of radical autonomy, that the secular city (*civitas terrena*) is what St. Augustine said it was—"a society motivated chiefly by *self*-love"—and, consequently, inherently *inhumane*. The emancipation of men from their bondages in nature and authoritarian societies of various sorts has now had time enough for preliminary testing of those heady promises of the prophets of autonomy as to what man could make of man if only he had the freedom and the challenge. Only a humanist bigot could claim that the results to date are reassuring. Only a theocratic bigot would wish for a return to the ghastly days of "Throne and Altar."

But this much is clear: technopolis is an unfit habitation for mankind unless it becomes vastly more *humane* than any part of it that we know now. The very size of mass communities militates against humane-ness so long as the chief bonds of those communities are self-love and "enlightened self-interest." The future of mankind gets darker rather than brighter if our hopes are built on the resources of human altruism within the moral atmosphere of *any* of the secular ideologies now bidding for man's allegiance.

The world is perishing for lack of the sort of environing love that *is* disinterested, that does not "intervene" or dominate, that turns men's hearts outward toward the neighbor, that suffers and struggles against man's inhumanity to man. But this is another way of pointing to the very nerve of the Christian tradition: God's *agape*, his love of creation and humanity. All of the other modes of God's presence in the world are summed up in this: this *is* what *he* is! His *agape* is his motive for providing a world to begin with; his love for the world so provided is what prompted the Incarnation of his love in Jesus Christ.

The Christian tradition has a word for this *agape* at work—this divine presence in human affairs. It is *charis* ("grace") and it is the mainspring of any proper Christian doctrine of providence. *Charis* affirms God's reality as the Provider of "heaven and earth," and it describes the character of his providence in human history and destiny. *Charis* is God's free, unfaltering love of nature (order and fruition) and his free, unmerited love for human history (the creature's *participation* in the earthly enterprises of grace). *Charis* is neither "substantial" nor "insubstantial." It is the affect in us of God's loyal love for us—the paradigm of which is his providence in Jesus Christ.

God's grace in nature is his judgment that all the things he holds in being are *good*, in and for themselves, that his mercy is over *all* his works, that men are stewards and trustees of God's good world and, therefore, under the moral imperative to cherish, conserve, and augment the world's well-being and joy in well-being. In this respect, the religion of God's grace is a thoroughly worldly religion, which is corrupted whenever it repudiates or scorns the world, whenever it neglects any suitable occasion for celebrating and serving worldly values.

God's grace is also evident in history in the far more baffling mystery of sin and tragic freedom, in the mystery of reconciliation and communion. History is the record of what man has made of his human possibilities. Read one way, it is a sorry story. There is, however, another reading—of grace as God's unfailing care for his creatures despite their wayward and demonic alienations. History, thus, is the record of man's pathos and predicament and of God's ceaseless wrestling with us—not to cancel our freedom but to bless us if only by thwarting our sins from ever coming to any final triumph. Grace is the most fully human mode of God's presence in human history—the sign and the agency of his providence and promise in and for *this* world. One might hope that some such "traditional" view as this of God-with-us in nature and history would come nearer to meeting the *good intentions* of the "radicals" than the implicates of their own reckless rejections of the Christian tradition.

III
Providence as Presence

In the first pagan world into which Christianity went, there were gods all over the place—as St. Paul noticed in Athens—bright Olympian gods (and goddesses, of course) with their lively immoralities, dark chthonian gods (and goddesses) with their mysterious powers in "nature" and the life-processes. Paul's observation about the Athenians—that they were "*very* religious," with even an altar "to the unknown god," just in case!—would have held good, in greater or less degree, for popular religion anywhere in the Graeco-Roman world.

But the over-all impact of the pagan pantheon on the faithful was something close to a reign of terror. The sky deities (the first jet-set?) were whimsical at best—and men were more often victims than beneficiaries of their celestial hi-jinks. The earth deities were as insatiable as the life-forces they controlled—and as irrational. Beyond them all were the faceless arbiters of destiny: Fate, Fortune, and Happenstance (*Tuchē*). It was in conscientious disbelief that human existence was at the mercy of such divine psychopaths that the Greek philosophical religions developed their alternate wisdoms about life: Platonism, Stoicism, Epicureanism, Plotinism. For all their differences, these several systems had two common aims: (1) to ease man's terror of the divine by re-conceiving the cosmos in moral and rational terms and (2) to offer men ways of salvation that promised human dignity, freedom, and happiness. Their slogans for the ideal condition ("apathy" for the Stoics, "ataraxy" for the Epicureans—both best translated as "serenity") are vivid clues to the ghastly anguish and anxieties chronic in popular "religion," from which "philosophy" gave hope of redemption. All of them preached a gospel of self-knowledge, self-control, self-fulfillment, based on a rational understanding of the human possibility. For the Stoics, existence was set in a framework of "law," rational and benevolent, yet rigid and impersonal. Men find their happiness in their *self*-disciplined conformity to reason and the rule of natural law. For the Epicureans, the fear of the gods was the beginning of *un*wisdom. Salvation begins as men cast away their fears; it continues as they learn the dignified avoidance of pain and the rational cultivation of pleasure (what Freud, later on, would call "the pleasure principle"). The Platonists taught men to contemplate, and urged them to participate in, the ideal order of beauty, truth, and goodness.

In both Platonism and Stoicism there were multiple versions of a concept of divine *pronoia* (foreknowledge) and *prothesis* (purpose) based on the eternal pre-existence of the forms and forces that make the good life possible. For the Platonists, there are the forms (the realm of ideas and rational pattern—what Whitehead called "the eternal objects"). Then there was "the Receptacle" (matter), the matrix which "accepted" the forms for actualization. Finally, there was the eternal Agent who wrought the forms into phenomena as perfectly as possible. The life of wisdom consists in the awareness of the real within the realm of shadows and the love of "being" in all its manifestations. The summative Form of all the forms is the Good. This means that the value-tone of all real being is good and, therefore, that life is good as men participate in this ambient goodness.

For the Stoics, the eternal providence was rather like the script of the cosmic cycles through which world history proceeds unfolding scene by scene—so that men cannot see the whole (save in a sort of cyclic retrospect) but can at least find their own roles in the drama and play them with dignity and self-control.

Greek Christians, preaching the apostolic Gospel to Greek pagans in an atmosphere in which religion was nerve-wracking and philosophy abstract, had many problems on their hands. The original form of the Gospel and all its presuppositions were Jewish. The ethical monotheism which the Jews had achieved so painfully—and which they saw threatened by the Christian worship of Jesus Christ as "Lord and Savior"—was the foundation of the Christian world-view, and it cut across the various pagan ideologies at an odd angle. It asserted that the world was governed and man's destiny guided by the righteous will of the Creator-God, which sounded like yet another of the religious mythologies. And yet this governing will of God (his "Kingdom") was conceived to be utterly good and fully concerned with *human blessedness*, which sounded like another "philosophy." Moreover, the Christian definition of blessedness always connoted the realization of the human possibility—provided by the God-Father, exhibited by the God-Man, developed by the indwelling Paraclete. The Christian God was not a god of the gaps but the God of the givens—the Giver of *every* good and perfect gift (cf. James 1:17). The reach of his care for his creation and his human creatures stretched out to the trivial (numbered hairs and falling sparrows), down to the depths of human self-abandonment (the Cross and the "harrowing of hell"), up and beyond to the final vindication of the rule of righteousness (". . . and he shall come again in glory to judge the living and the dead"). The Christian story—biblical foundations, liturgical celebrations, theological interpretations—was all ordered around the central theme of God's gracious "presence" in all creation, history, and human destiny. God in his inner reality was unknown and unknowable. When Christian theologians spoke of him as "doing" this or "being" there, their language was usually less often "mythological" (in the pagan sense) than *apophatic:* sentences that affirm significant truths in indicative statements whose *literal* meaning is also denied—all at the same time. For example,

> The eternal God is our refuge,
> And underneath are the everlasting arms.
> [cf. Deut. 33:27]

Taken literally, this is nonsense. To speak of it as "mythological" leads to endless ambiguities and negations. To understand it apophatically allows us to take it seriously, critically, *and in context.* Some such distinction is utterly crucial for any valid reading of the biblical and patristic texts—as the confusion about demythologizing has reminded us.

The trouble was that the biblical vocabulary differed from that of the philosophers. The philosophers' favorite term for the divine governance of the world was *pronoia*, but this word occurs only once in the Septuagint—in the Apocrypha at that (Wis. Sol. 6:7)—in the sense of God's wise and benevolent care for all creatures great and small. There are two instances of *pronoia* in the New Testament, but they refer to human arrangements for special events. There are the cognate terms, *proginōskō* and *prognosis*, but their only references to God are to his fore-ordination of Christ as Savior (cf. I Peter 1:20) and to his "definite plan and foreknowledge" of man's salvation through Christ (cf. Acts 2:23). The nearest we come to a biblical term for providence is *prothesis*. Five times (Rom. 8:28, 9:11; Eph. 1:11, 3:11; II Tim. 1:9) it denotes God's "purpose" which "is everywhere at work" (Eph. 1:11) and which has already been "achieved in Christ Jesus our Lord" (3:11). Our salvation is not on account of our own merit but through God's "purpose and grace" (II Tim. 1:9)—note here the easy yoking of *prothesis* and *charis*!

There is, however, one unusual usage of *prothesis* that has often struck me as an implicit reference to God's providence in a rather special way. This is the phrase, "shewbread" (KJV) or "Bread of the Presence" (Matt. 12:4; Mark 2:26; Luke 6:4; Heb. 9:2, RSV). The reference here is to the twelve consecrated loaves exhibited in the sanctuary and reserved for the priests (Ex. 25:30; Lev. 24:5-9) which David and his troops commandeered as emergency rations (I Sam. 21:6). Was this a relic of earlier pagan offerings of human "provisions" to feed the gods or was it the transformation of such a relic into an exemplary symbol of *God's provision* of the staff of life—i.e. that life thus sustained is sacred to God? Jesus' use of the story—as well as the reference in Hebrews—suggests the latter. If so, we are close to the nerve of the petition in the Lord's Prayer, "Give us this day our daily bread": the acknowledgment of God as Provider of the common necessities of the daily round.

In the Graeco-Roman world, therefore, the Christian message of a personal God—"whose mercy is over *all* his works"—was all too easily construed in terms of a divine genie, who manipulated the twists and turns of nature and history; for in that mind-set, "nature" was fully as erratic and unpredictable as human behavior. And so the Christian God became more readily identified by miracles, angelic visitations, and episodic interventions than by his constant spiritual presence in human hearts and community. In those days such transcendental views passed for sophistication. The contrary notion of the immanence of the most high God—directly involved in this disgusting world—was repulsive to many a sensitive or speculative soul for whom the problem of evil was thus made utterly insoluble. And so arose the first reformers and revisionists—Marcion and the Gnostics—with their gospels of pure *agape*, pure transcendence, pure spirituality. The orthodox Christian defense against these attractive "heresies" amounted to a reassertion of the radical secularity of the Gospel: God the creator and all-governing Father, his full involvement in man's lot in Christ on the Cross, the pervasive immanence of his Holy Spirit in the Christian community at work and worship. What was at stake in the Gnostic controversy was not the fantastic cosmogonic speculations that the Gnostics spun out—emanations of aeons and syzygies, etc., etc.—but rather the question whether Christians ought to abandon their conviction about God's real presence in *this* world: *to* nature and *for* humanity. The Christian choice was to suffer the embarrassments of a secular gospel in order to hold intact their original faith in the one God who is at once Creator, Redeemer, Inspirer.

But over against the prevailing cosmologies that saw the world dominated by sheer chance and blind fate, Christians had to assert God's *orderly* and *moral* governance of creation. Here they made common cause with the Stoics and Platonists in arguing that the basic purpose (*prothesis*) of existence is the support and vindication of truth and righteousness. The cosmic struggle between the good God and the demons (Satan, Devil, Lucifer, etc.) became a plausible model for interpreting human affairs—and the history of the church! Lactantius and the early church historians saw the providence of God chiefly in the miraculous preservation of the Christian community against overwhelming odds, in the dismal end of "bad" emperors and the glorious memories of the good ones. Salvianus took the accusations of the Roman pagans that Rome's downfall was due to the Christians and gave it an ironic twist: Rome's disasters were God's judgment against the Christians for their failures in not making more of their opportunities to reform Roman society. Christian historiography, from Eusebius to Baronius, has a common heuristic theme: the powers of good and evil in endless conflict, with the human arena as battleground.

Because, to the pagan mind, the gods were so threatening, there was a powerful impulse to take refuge from divine whimsy, to conceive of a strict duality that separated good from evil, spirit from matter, infinitude from finite process. Thus, the idealists denied that the high God was involved in or responsible for the actual world. But the Christians were "stuck" with their conviction that God is not absent anywhere. For them, the whole creation is sacral through and through (because of God's providence) and yet also secular throughout (because of man's responsibilities). From this laudable co-inherence, however, there then developed a widespread and fatal misconstruction: the dominance of the secular order by the sacerdotal. As the church sought to civilize the feudal society which was never much more than a poorly organized reign of terror, it resorted to the pretensions of theocracy. As the feudal society sought to domesticate the church, the realms of "sacred" and "secular" were set in bitter rivalry. On the surface, the messy conflict seems mainly political. But there was a far deeper issue: does the sovereignty of God reach to the marrow of human politics and to life in the *saeculum* (*this* world)? This issue was hopelessly corrupted when both sides agreed that what was "secular" was not "sacred" and vice versa—and then fought over the dividing line! This false disjunction still plagues us.

St. Augustine had made the classical distinction—which Harvey Cox has now turned on its head—between the *civitas terrena* (human society organized by self-love and its moral implicates) and the *civitas Dei* (society organized by the love of God above all else and the love of all else in God). The bishop of Hippo denied that God was absent from the secular city and he also avoided any simple identification of the heavenly city with the Catholic church. His main stress was on God's providential management of history on behalf of God's righteous rule in human culture.

St. Thomas labored to develop his notions of providence as management in support of his basic vision of God's governance of the entire creation—lovingly and with perfect wisdom—preserving it in being by continuous creation, enforcing the concurrence of the natural, the rational, and the moral by the tranquil operation of his eternal counsels—and yet also by fresh creative acts that enlarge the scope of created possibilities.

When the Protestants came finally to develop philosophical systems as buttresses for their fideistic theologies, they followed the basic Reformation line of exalting grace and subordinating creation, thus shifting the emphasis from natural revelation to God's specific revelation in Jesus Christ. Even so, they kept intact the traditional concepts of providence as divine management (if only by remote control and occasional intervention). Here is a typical sample from the Calvinist tradition:

> The acts of Providence are three:
> (1) He preserves all things in their being and duration;
> (2) He moves all things to their action by concurrence, in fact by precurrence;
> (3) He steers and guides all things to the desired end to which they were appointed from eternity.[1]

This special emphasis on concurrent intervention has

1. Johannes Braun, *A Didactic and Cogent System of Theology* (Amsterdam, 1688), I, 12, 2. Quoted in Heinrich Heppe (ed.), *Reformed Dogmatics* (London: George Allen & Unwin, Ltd., 1950), p. 256.

continued in the Calvinist tradition down to our own times. James McCosh, one of the great bridge builders between Scottish and American Presbyterianism in the nineteenth century entitled his major treatise *The Method of Divine Government, Physical and Moral* (1869). Another stalwart in that same tradition, Charles Hodge, developed a similar view in his *Systematic Theology* (1888)[2]—which is still in print, and still in use as a textbook in conservative seminaries. As recently as 1952, Professor Gerrit Berkouwer, of the Free University of Amsterdam, published a careful review of the arguments of Herman Bavinck, Abraham Kuyper, and Herman Dooyeweerd on the merits and demerits of the idea of providence as current intervention.[3]

The classical Anglican teaching on providence affirmed the idea of concurrence as a matter of course, but the stress tended to fall on the affects of grace in creation, especially in the forum of human freedom. William Sherlock's *Discourse Concerning the Divine Providence* (1694) can serve as an exemplar of the whole tradition:

> The general notion of Providence is God's care of all the creatures he has made, which must consist in preserving and upholding their beings and natures, and in such acts of government as the good order of the world and the happiness of mankind require. . . . (p. 19)

> God had endowed all creatures with such natural powers and virtues as may answer for the ends for which they were made . . . and [he] established a natural concourse and co-operation to actuate all the

2. Cf. I, p. 616.
3. *The Providence of God* (Grand Rapids: Wm. B. Eerdmans).

> powers of nature, by a perpetual law, which is that blessing God bestowed upon all creatures at the time of creation. (p. 27)
>
> . . . But in the government of mankind, God exercises a very different power over the minds of men. He changes [their] hearts and counsels, imprints new thoughts upon their minds, claps a new bias upon their wills and affections. . . . He renews and sanctifies good men by his Spirit, enlightens their understandings, . . . inspires them with divine affections. He gives up bad men to . . . their own affected ignorance, blindness, inconsideration, to the obstinacy and perverseness of their own wills and to the empire of their lusts. . . . This improves and heightens and regulates our faculties, enlarges our knowledge and rectifies our choices, and directs and governs our passions. (pp. 29–30)

In the old paganism, where the divine presence was assumed—but usually as arbitrary or mischievous—the task of Christian teaching was to stress God's utter trustworthiness, his gracious and competent benevolence. Now the tables are turned because the presuppositions have altered. In the new paganism it is the divine absence that is assumed. This change of climate transforms the program, though not the goal, of the Christian apologist. Now, he must argue for benevolent "presence" without arbitrary "intervention," which means fighting on two fronts (since the old paganism still has powerful residues even in the "modern" mentality). We can see the resulting perplexities of this new undertaking in recent theology when it dares to speak of providence at all (which is not often). Professor L. E. Elliott-Binns tackles the challenge hopefully but with a cautious conclusion:

> We are to think of God or Providence as both above time yet as working in time, and of ourselves as co-operating with Him towards the great end for which the universe was created. From the contemplation of His acts in time we may rise to some knowledge of His eternal purposes, the true substance of which all human endeavors are but the reflection.[4]

Professor Roger Hazelton is more sensitive to the modern mood and more sophisticated in his positive approach:

> If we are going to reconstitute the idiom and idea of Providence in our time, we must first identify ourselves with [the skeptics] in those very situations of lostness, dread, or emptiness where the thought of a guiding, guarding, governing God is being sharply questioned.
>
> We do this best . . . by coming at the doctrine of providence not systematically but strategically, by trying to see God at work in just those experiences from which he seems to be evacuated. We must, I think, permit our belief to shine through the darkness of our doubt. That is, in fact, the genius of this particular doctrine.[5]

Paul Tillich's section on "historical Providence" in his *Systematic Theology* (III, 372-74) is uncharacteristically brief and cautious—almost half-hearted. The burden of his thesis is:

> God's directing creativity works through the spontaneity of creatures and human freedom. . . . Historical providence includes all this and is creative

4. L. E. Elliott-Binns, *Divine Providence and Human Destiny* (London: Society for Promoting Christian Knowledge, 1943), p. 86.
5. Roger Hazelton, *God's Way with Man; Variations on the Theme of Providence* (New York: Abingdon Press, 1956), p. 6.

> through it toward the new, both in history and above history. . . . The way in which this happens is identical with the divine mystery and beyond calculation and description. . . .

One of the most resolute responses to the challenge of incredulity may be found in W. G. Pollard's *Chance and Providence* (1958) where the clue is given in the sub-title, *God's Action in a World Governed by Scientific Law.* Dr. Pollard, a distinguished physicist (and an ordained Episcopal priest), believes that "biblical Providence and scientific causality" can be reconciled. He focuses on the radical duality

> between chance and accident as seen in science [its arbitrary and "uncertain" phenomena] and providence as seen in the Bible [profoundly personal]. . . . [This duality] reveals to us in a decisive and illuminating way how and why it is that the methods of science can never penetrate beyond chance and accident to discover any evidence of providence, and at the same time how and why it should be that the hand of God in history can only be known, as the Church has always maintained, through revelation. . . . This insight also shows us . . . [why] . . . the same sequence of events can be apprehended by one observer as merely a remarkable streak of luck while being recognized by another for what it really is: a mighty act of the living God. The reason is that the subject-object and person-person relationships are not two separate worlds but two aspects of a single total reality.[6]

The twin perplexities in these efforts to conserve and

6. William G. Pollard, *Chance and Providence; God's Action in a World Governed by Scientific Law* (New York: Charles Scribner's Sons, 1958), pp. 170–171.

restate the traditional views of providence is that they all tend to conflate the domains of nature, history, and spiritual community (church) and to construe providence in terms of causal activity—which would be appropriate to *nature* alone, if it is allowable anywhere at all. What, then, if we have already declined the notion of God as a causal factor in nature as incredible—because we have seen that the natural order, both past and future, is consistently determinate? If we have agreed that non-intervention in nature is to be taken for granted, then much that has accrued to the traditional doctrines of Providence has to be put aside, whether quietly or defiantly. Indeed, this seems to be the juiciest bone of contention between the radicals and the traditionalists in the current hubbub. One thing is clear: we are past the point (were past it long ago without admitting it) when we can any longer argue for a doctrine that portrays providence as a divine genie, favoring the favored, or unrolling the script of history, with sneak previews provided in the Scriptures as a special service for the sharp-eyed and knowledgeable.

One might wish that we could simply shed the baggage of overbelief in God as an immanent cause in natural process without having to deny the embarrassing charge of reductionism. Surely this was the main point to Bultmann's demythologizing program. This would have the double advantage of reducing the unedifying effort of trying to reconcile the scientific views of the biblical writers with the knowledge of our salvation and of voiding those useless efforts at finding gaps into which God may still be slotted. This is rear-guard apologetics and rear-guards, however heroic, are there to be expended and usually are.

We can find safer and more solid ground in the notion that the idea of providence as concurrent intervention is not rigorously required for Christian faith, by either the biblical revelation or by Christian insights into the mystery of salvation, as these have developed through the centuries. The living substance of what *is* testified in Scripture and what *must* be explicated by Christian thought is the sovereignty, freedom and grace of the triune God—from the Father through the Son in the Holy Spirit. This can best be done by the frank recognition that the sovereignty of God is manifest more edifyingly in order than in accident—and this is certainly the case in the contemporary climate where men have increasing confidence that nature is a uniform cosmos and not a constellation of "accidents" (as seemed obvious to our forefathers). Where there are real gaps that threaten real chaos, God's sovereignty must cover those gaps or else be stultified—and this is what the traditional doctrines of providence did. But are there such gaps in a world-view that can envisage a unified field-theory? Again, where the *cosmos* is conceived (as by the Stoics and too many traditionalist Christians) as a prefabricated rigid order (impersonal, inexorable, uncaring), there is need for asserting God's gracious and personal presence throughout the creation. For the doctrine of providence has never been more or less, by intention at least, than a recognition of the myriad ways in which God's Provident Mystery makes possible the well-being of his creatures and guides them in their own processes of self-fulfillment which includes, of course, the effects of active grace in the "moments" of real freedom.

If nature is determinate in both its past and future, then God's providence for it is to be recognized in his provision for dynamic process and creative evolution—or however else we may come to conceive the idea of nature. God's presence in the natural order is neither as artificer nor engineer but as the provider of the aboriginal possibilities of natural occurrence (Whitehead's "primordial nature" of God) and as the sustaining matrix of the process in which these possibilities are realized or aborted (God's "consequent nature"). When "God saw everything that he had made, and behold, it was *very* good," this was the divine seal of approval on the enterprise and its prospects. This is not the deist notion of the creator who sets the works in motion and then sits back to wait until something goes awry. The creation was *de nihilo* and still is. Nothing in modern science supports the notion of the eternity of matter or of cosmological prefabrication. But the creation is also *constant.* And this is the decisive quality and character of God's presence in nature: the provision and maintenance of dynamic order in a constant and trustworthy cosmos. This order is far from fully known as yet—one suspects that man's scientific reach will forever exceed his grasp—but the pre-supposition that it is knowable at all points to the ground of intelligibility itself: the ordering environment of the ordered environment that we know.

It is not required of the working scientist that he know or name the "providence" of this ordering environment. And it is crucial that, as a philosopher of *science,* he should exclude any such idea from his "working hypotheses" about causality within the ordered environment. But it is equally crucial that he should not rule out the idea of a transcendent ground of order and energy in the name of some "naturalistic" *meta*physics, avowed or unavowed. Indeed, of all modern men, it is the scientists whose careers are most crucially staked on such "unprovables" as uniformity, continuity, mathematical constants, the integrity of truth, etc., etc. Sometimes I think that the scientists are the only true believers left in a skeptical age. They know as well as we the chance and random data in their fields, but they never suppose that these lie outside the scope of theoretical inclusion—and they instinctively mistrust any theory of *random* action. This means that they can live and work in confidence and without *hubris*—which could serve as one definition of *faith*!

But we must still try to conceive the reality of God's active presence in the world and in human affairs without sneaking the *deus ex machina* back onto the stage in a new costume and mask. The crucial distinction, I should think, lies between any notion of God as an immanent cause *in* space and time (one cause among many) and the idea of God as the immanent influence of love and goodness in those "moments" when man's freedom, intelligence, and power to love issue in spontaneous "decisions" that transvalue the meanings of past and mutate the prospects of the human future. These "moments" of freedom, we have already argued, are outside the causal order but within our human "lifetimes." They do not compete with clock-time; what they do is to "measure" its existential significance. God's immanence is his presence in human "times-present."

We have also suggested that all serious "God-talk" is apophatic and parabolic—best understood not in syllogistic conclusions but through analogies and parables which prompt *insights* that allow for rational reflection. And the most illuminating analogy in our culture for "explaining" the influence of the immanence of purposive love in the crises of human freedom may be seen in those healing insights that come in the course of successful psychotherapy, which is yet another way of observing the mystery of memory, contuition and hope.

Consider the meaning of human freedom in the psychotherapeutic situation. For the psychologically disabled—and this holds true in moral and "spiritual" disorders, as well—a "correct" diagnosis imposed from without is as unhelpful as an incorrect diagnosis. This was Paul's point in Romans 7! Any good psychotherapist can recognize "what's wrong" long before the patient does but he cannot effect a cure forthwith by direct intervention, as an internist or a surgeon might. He knows that something far more complicated and unmanageable is involved. Symptoms can be reduced, of course, and much mitigation of anxieties, depressions, and social disruption. Moreover, the new opening psychodelic frontiers (in responsible medicine, that is, not Haight-Ashbury!) give promise of horizons of manipulating human consciousness that outdistance the boldest apocalypses of the mystics. Even so, the essence of any genuine psychotherapeutic *cure* ("wholeness" recovered or achieved) remains what it always was: *self-understanding*—i.e. new and more valid insights concerning the patient's own identity and capacities, his own psychodynamic development and deviations, the cosmos or chaos of his own interpersonal relations, *his* realistic prospects in a future that he can accept without neurotic evasion. Such self-understanding can rarely be achieved, if ever, "on one's own," or in the patient's "normal" interpersonal situation. What is needed is significant *personal presence*, intelligent and honest, equally concerned for the *patient's* problems *as they have been experienced* by him, and for the claims and possibilities of reality, as these may be rationally assessed. Cure comes by insight; insights are "given" in an atmosphere of intelligent love—and there is never a specific cause for any particular insight. Real re-entry into one's past—in contrast to the pat rehearsals of biased recollections that neurotics usually begin with—is very difficult. Crucial breakthroughs come, when they do, in "flashes" or even in dreams, etc. Self-chosen change (*repentance*!)—in contrast to remorse or self-justification—is also a very tricky business, involving emotional re-attachments to the therapist and others that must be handled with delicacy and skill. This is why the transference phenomenon, and its handling, is the crux of every psychiatric case history.

Such healing requires time for maturation and freedom from even the best-intentioned manipulation. And it also requires a *personal presence*—a special sort of spiritual relation that is loving without being selfish, and understanding without being officious. This presence has also to be sensed by the patient for what it is, and trusted without dependence or resentment. Psychological healing is a *synergism* between the freedom of the patient (crippled or corrupted as it may be) and the providence of the doctor (as partial and imperfect as that may be)—both in an atmosphere of the love and mutual respect that Christians call "grace."

It is worth repeating that significant insights don't just happen and they do not turn up as direct conclusions of linear reasoning. They require a context of freedom and rational inquiry. They are "spontaneous" but not without background; they are also cumulative, and their practical consequences must be followed up or else they quickly spoil. And they rarely come in the course of didactic comments or coaching, however wise and well-meant. The good therapist is, above all else, a good listener. He is not at all passive but his impulses to intervene are under the control of his judgment as how best to help the other find his own upright stance, to accept responsibility for himself and his future. It is this sort of *love* that creates the *presence* in which healing can happen. It is the antithesis of that self-regarding love that feels bound to "intervene."

There is more than a metaphorical analogy between this experience of the provident presence of human love and our faith-knowledge of God's providence. Christian experience in all its variety testifies to the felt presence of God's suffusing love that bestows freedom as a gift, that sustains us in our use and abuse of it, that comes to us in Christ ("the man of God's own choosing") to reveal the fullness of love, that reveals and enacts his purpose to salvage and perfect our humanity.

There is also, of course, a vivid danger of misunderstanding parables like this. One might somewhat too readily think of God as a bearded spook listening patiently to our narcissist rehearsals and our muffled cries for help.

The barrier between the biblical picture of the Living God as the sustaining environment of our existence and the animistic sense of God's magical providence as the Man Upstairs is very tenuous. There is no foolproof guard against man's incontinent idolatry. Idolatry is the worship of the creature—*any* creature: effigy, book, or whatever. It is, of course, the oldest and most cherished of all the ways in which men seek and assert their radical autonomy—for the man who makes an idol retains *some* measure of mastery even when he has enslaved himself to it. And, obviously, beyond the staple idolatries of blood and soil and ideology, there is the subtler one that tries to bring the One God Almighty within the grasp and management of special God-talkers and God-handlers.

It is against this oldest idolatry that the newest paganism has launched its most effective campaign. It has been greatly aided in this by the pervasive, tragic sense of God-forsakenness that has settled like smog in our "modern" minds, that tortures us like a lingering, unhealthy grief. The God-talkers and the God-handlers are increasingly mistrusted; more and more "modern" men feel bereft and deeply alienated. This bereavement has been tragically reinforced by the violence with which, once we had banished or buried the *dei ex machinae*, we rebounded into an opposite infatuation: the militant desacralization of *all* existence. Now we have sort of a general anaesthesia of our sense of the Holy, a numbing of our awareness of Encompassing Mystery. There was a time when the moral substance of Christianity was love of God *and* neighbor. Now there are those who believe that only the neighbor is left.

But there is a grim consequence to this one-sided choice, as we have begun to see: presently even the love of neighbor will go, too.

The evidence has been piling up for more than a century that reverence for humanity will not survive the loss of the conviction that personality is sacred—and yet the only steady ground this conviction has ever had is the faith that every man is priceless in God's sight, that human existence is sacred because God has sealed it with his love. Man's penchant for inhumanity is bad enough at best and this has all too often been made worse by invocations of deity. Now we are in the early stages of discovering what man's inhumanity to man amounts to when it is justified by avowedly humanitarian values—with *1984* still in the offing!

And so it turns out that this audacious concern to justify the ways of God to men is less for his sake than for our own. God-forsaking men are in mortal peril of having their own humanity diminished. And, in a world where nature is regarded as our ultimate providence the human venture itself becomes more and more absurd—for then our endless hunger for self-transcendence is forever self-defeating.

This, then, is why the Christians, from the beginning, have invited their fellow men to respond in authentic faith to the Provident Mystery that all men glimpse but otherwise misconstrue. The earliest sample of such an invitation is the summary of a sermon preached in Athens in the very first generation after Pentecost:

> The God who created the world and everything in it, and who is Lord of heaven and earth, does not

> live in shrines made by men. It is not because he lacks anything that he accepts service at men's hands, for he is himself *the universal giver* of life and breath and all else. He created every race of men of one stock, to inhabit the whole earth's surface. He fixed the epochs of their history and the limits of their territory. They were to seek God, and, it might be, touch and find him; though indeed he is not far from each one of us, for in him we live and move, in him we exist; as some of your own poets have said, "We are also his offspring." As God's offspring, then, we ought not to suppose that the deity is like an image in gold or silver or stone, shaped by human craftsmanship and design. As for the times of ignorance, God has overlooked them; but now he commands mankind, all men everywhere, to repent, because he has fixed the day on which he will have the world judged, and justly judged, by a man of his choosing; of this he has given assurance to all by raising him from the dead. [Acts 17:24–31, NEB]

Here are the bare bones of the notion of providence that we are trying to understand and to commend as still credible and relevant.

It argues, in effect, that God is purposively present in human existence as the Creator and Provider of the human possibility, as the Lawgiver who rightfully demands that men live reverently and righteously in communion with him and one another, as the Inspirer of prophecy and Messianic hope, as the Incarnate Word, as the Holy Spirit who is building the ideal community in the midst of the human community and who preserves the ideal as a fresh possibility for each new and upcoming generation against the ravages of time. Providence is the sum of all the modes of his self-disclosure in human history, of all the effects of his love in our lives.

To perceive God's gracious presence and to respond appropriately is the very essence of worship, from the simplest prayer to the most elaborate Eucharist. To live in the acknowledged providence of God is to confess his judgment and mercy and grace, to accept his gift (provision) of reconciling love, to put one's final faith and hope in his grace, to find the lodestone for responsible ethical decision in his *agape*. And *this*, or something like it, is what the Christian tradition has called "salvation."

God's providence in nature is his provision for its order and energy-systems and for their integration. This is not a scientific hypothesis; it can neither be verified or falsified. It would be enough if "modern" men, immersed from birth in the scientific method and hope, could recognize it as an allowable *insight* in their own moments of primal wonder about life's meaning. For then the option of faith would remain alive and this is the only precondition that the Christian apologist rightly needs for significant dialogue between "science" and "religion."

God's providence in history is not as a meddling director nor yet as an absentee landlord, but rather as history's Assessor: the provider of those meanings and purposes that are worthily human. He is the first and final judge of the human performance, the redeemer who restores meanings that have been spoiled, the consummator who holds the future open, against all odds, for the eventual triumph of righteousness.

The exhibition of the specifically human dimension of God's provident presence is in Jesus Christ. Here, in a human life with cosmic consequences, we may decipher God's eternal purpose in and for the human enterprise, his mode of presenting his law and his love to men desperately estranged from both, his way of coping with sin and evil, the manifestation of his power and wisdom, his "opening of the Kingdom of Heaven to all believers." In Jesus Christ, we have to do with the Living God's revelation of what all other revelations of God, wherever and whenever, really mean. In Jesus Christ, we have also to do with one of our very own humankind, in a summary revelation of what all other revelations of humanity amount to.

It is tempting, of course, to find the signs of a special providence in history in its odd turns and "accidents"—or to look for it in the gaps that dot the historian's story. But if God is anywhere at all, it must surely be in his provision for the whole: in continuity and discontinuity, in the routine and the extraordinary, in the systolic-diastolic rhythms of crisis and perdurance. His purpose in it all—not coercive and yet not merely casual—is that men should rise above and beyond their own self-centered purviews of life and that, from such fresh perspectives, they may gain more wisdom, modesty and self-reliant courage "for the living of these days."

When, then, we speak of divine providence and purpose in Christian terms, we are trying to point to God's provision for the processes and prospects of the human enterprise. We are confessing our belief in God's resourcefulness in his dealings with any and all his human creatures, his unfaltering love in sustaining them in their wayward histories and his pardoning mercy in salvaging their corrupted aims and hopes. Providence does not mean the divine predetermination of historical events. It means rather the provision that such events may be affected by reason, grace, and hope. It means the provision of a community of faith and grace in which men may cultivate their consciousness of God's presence and imperative love, in Word and Sacrament, in faithful witness and sacrificial service.

In some such terms as these, men may ponder the history of God's providential care for his people in their groping pilgrimages through time and space and waywardness. They may see in the survival of the church through her perennial crises a warrant for doubting that she is finally done for yet. They might very well discover, in the ambiguous records of the Christian past, the secret of Christian poise in a time of panic—i.e. perspective! And, finally, they might learn really to believe the witness of the saints, attested in life and death, that *nothing* in all creation can separate God's faithful children from his deathless love in Christ Jesus our Lord.

IV

God's Providence and Man's Anguish

There is, of course, no blinking the fact that even so mildly cheerful a view of God's providence as we have been expounding falls afoul of human anguish—suffering, tragedy, sin, and the fear of death. Here is the stone of stumbling for all those blithe spirits who can, upon occasion, keep singing past the first stanza of "This Is My Father's World."

Existence *is* untoward—it is "thrown," "broken," and experienced as an agony. Any thoughtful man might well imagine that he could have devised a cosmic operation less replete with frustration, suffering, and indignity. And this, for Christians, has been a perennial torment, for the fact of evil brings God's good name into doubt. It is a hazard to belief, a temptation to disbelief. How can it be true that God's sovereign love is "present" in the carnage and wastage of *this* world?

Interestingly enough, this question got its classic form—*whence* evil? (*unde est malum?*)—from the pagan theologians and philosophers, whose answers reflect their several theologies. In the teachings of the popular religions, evil was regarded as a by-product: of the careless antics of the sky-gods or the purposeful cruelties of the earth-gods. In either case, the gods, preoccupied with their own affairs, were not themselves affected by the mischief or misery they wreaked. The religious philosophers from Socrates to Plotinus rightly regarded such notions as profoundly immoral—and said so. This is why Socrates was executed as an atheist and why, in return, Plato barred "the poets" (spokesmen for the popular mythologies) from his ideal community. For the Platonists, evil was identified as the privation or corruption of the good (itself identified with being). For the Stoics, it was the harvest of unreason and the lack of self-control. For the Epicureans, it was the blind way of the world from which the wise man withdraws as far as possible. In each case, the common effect of these "theodicies" was to disengage the divine from the hurlyburly of ordinary life and to propose a program of aloofness as the right answer to the problem: the mystic way of the Platonists, the way of reason for the Stoics, the way of serene indifference of the Epicureans.

The case stood quite differently with the Christians, who were stuck with their faith in God's sovereign providence in the whole creation, "warts and all." The Old Testament is full of tales of God's complicity in discreditable affairs, and yet it never disavows his final responsibility for the world and its ways. Indeed, this was the scandal that drove the very first "radical theologian" in the Christian ranks (Marcion) to his desperate efforts to rescue the true Gospel of Love (which he found in his own expurgated canon of the Pauline letters) from its fatal corruption in what by his time had become "traditional Christianity." The Gnostics were able to shake the Christian community to its foundations with their claim that their doctrines cleared the High God's name from any association with the creator of this earthly shambles. This challenge forced the church into one of its profoundest crises. On the one hand, God had to be cleared of the charge that he was the author of evil and sin, or else the Gospel of his sovereign goodness went down the cosmic drain. On the other hand, if dualism was the only recourse for preserving his goodness, then his provident involvement in creation would have to be abandoned. Orthodoxy staked its integrity on the conjunction of God's sovereignty *and* his goodness and thereby posed the question that has continued as perennial: how to maintain *both* in the face of man's universal experience of evil.

As usual, the Christians tried everything they could think of—in one or another of two main tendencies. In their liturgies and devotions the stress was on God's involvement—the Divine Sacrifice for which the Cross and Eucharist were the effective symbols. In their metaphysical reflections, however, the accent moved over to a stress on God's remotion from the finite. Men like Tertullian and Origen and, thereafter, the Cappadocians and Augustine, made much of God's transcendence, his invulnerability to change, passion, degradation—which is to say immutability, im-passibility, a-seity, etc., etc. (the "attributes" of deity so long familiar to the philosophers). What held these two divergent tendencies in fruitful tension was the Christian consensus on God's *com*passion. Moreover, the Christians were blocked off from either of the extremes of immanence or transcendence because of their prior commitment to the distinctive focus of their faith: the Incarnation of God's saving love and wisdom in Jesus of Nazareth.

Here again the ways divided. In Irenaeus and the Eastern theologians, there emerged a type of theodicy which began by accepting the reality of evil and of God's responsibility for its existence, together with a matching affirmation of the final triumph of grace over the interim powers of sin and death. In an excellent recent book, Professor John Hick has reviewed this Irenaean tradition carefully and uses it as the basis for a persuasive theodicy for moderns.

> Irenaeus sees our world of mingled good and evil as a divinely appointed environment for man's development towards the perfection that represents the fulfillment of God's good purpose for him.[1]

The other, and far more massive, tradition in theodicy was fashioned in and for Latin Christianity by Augustine, and it ran to the effect that while evil was existentially real enough—nobody ever denied *that*!—it had no essence of its own, no ontic ground. There is a definitive summary of this position in the *Enchiridion* (IV, 12, 13) which is as brief, and far clearer, than a paraphrase would be:

> All of nature, therefore, is good, since the Creator of all nature is supremely good. But nature is not supremely and immutably good as is the Creator of it. Thus the good in created things can be diminished and augmented. For good to be diminished is evil;

1. John Hick, *Evil and the God of Love* (London: The Macmillan Company, 1966), p. 221. The whole section on "The Irenaean Type of Theodicy," p. 207 ff. is worth very careful study.

still, however much it is diminished, something must remain of its original nature as long as it exists at all. For no matter what kind or however insignificant a thing may be, the good which is its "nature" cannot be destroyed without the thing itself being destroyed. There is good reason, therefore, to praise an uncorrupted thing, and if it were indeed an incorruptible thing which could not be destroyed, it would doubtless be all the more worthy of praise. When, however, a thing is corrupted, its corruption is an evil because it is, by just so much, a privation of the good. Where there is no privation of the good, there is no evil. Where there is evil, there is a corresponding diminution of the good. As long, then, as a thing is being corrupted, there is good in it of which it is being deprived; and in this process, if something of its being remains that cannot be further corrupted, this will then be an incorruptible entity [*natura incorruptibilis*], and to this great good it will have come through the process of corruption. But even if the corruption is not arrested, it still does not cease having some good of which it cannot be further deprived. If, however, the corruption comes to be total and entire, there is no good left either, because it is no longer an entity at all. Wherefore, corruption cannot consume the good without also consuming the thing itself. Every actual entity [*natura*] is therefore good; a greater good if it cannot be corrupted, a lesser good if it can be. Yet only the foolish and unknowing can deny that it is still good when wholly corrupted. Whenever a thing is consumed by corruption, not even the corruption remains, for it is nothing in itself, having no subsistent being in which to exist.

From this it follows that there is nothing to be called evil if there is nothing good. A good that

> wholly lacks an evil aspect is entirely good. Where there is some evil in a thing, its good is defective or defectible. Thus there can be no evil where there is no good. This leads us to a surprising conclusion: that, since every being, in so far as it is a being, is good, if we then say that a defective thing is bad, it would seem to mean that we are saying that what is evil is good, that only what is good is ever evil and that there is no evil apart from something good. This is because every actual entity is good [*omnis natura bonum est*]. Nothing evil exists *in itself*, but only as an evil aspect of some actual entity. Therefore, there can be nothing evil except something good. Absurd as this sounds, nevertheless the logical connections of the argument compel us to it as inevitable.[2]

This is a better argument, I think, than Professor Hick has found it to be.[3] It "explains" how God's grace can remain sovereign and undefeated even while it is being resisted and tainted. It shatters the force of the Manichaean dualism that had bemused Augustine himself and that remains a temptation to those who find it easy to take evil "at face value." It was consistent with the Gospel's promised remedy for the ravages of sin and it reinforced the Christian hope that, in the end, God would be "all in all" (I Cor. 15:28). It stresses, as the Irenaean tradition does not, the metaphysical chasm between being and non-being, between truth and error, between good as positive and evil as privative.

The general line of this Augustinian theodicy was followed in the West—and in the East from John of Damas-

2. *Augustine: Confessions and Enchiridion*, Library of Christian Classics (Philadelphia: The Westminister Press, 1955), Vol. VII, pp. 343–44.
3. *Op. cit.*, pp. 59–64.

cus—down through Aquinas and Calvin to Karl Barth and Austin Farrer, whose *Love Almighty and Ills Unlimited* is the best of its recent restatements—an "opposite number" to Professor Hick's book.

But it has two liabilities and they are serious. In the first place, it readily appears to a victim of evil as if it were explaining his ills away. Any actual experience of suffering, pain, or indignity is more likely to give rise to consternation, outrage or despair than to the serene realization that it is privative and ultimately unreal. So what if evil is only the corruption of the good? Are we less agonized by its horrid harvest of misery? Evil is felt as a positive *assault* against the good and it adds insult to injury to be told that the stimulus of our anguish is not really real. This privative notion has the merit of denying its antithesis—that God is absent from, or helpless in, these episodes of rampant evil. But its converse implicate—that God's providence is active in even the very worst that happens—is not easily remembered or believed when men are being shattered by natural disasters or degraded by sin and inhumanity.

In the second place, this Augustinian perspective complicates the doctrine of providence, to which it is vitally related. In defense of the sovereignty of grace—and this is its chief concern—it inserts the Plotinian notions of immutability and impassibility as necessary ingredients in such a sovereignty. In this view, the notion that God should "suffer" change or passion becomes unthinkable—equivalent to a denial of his power and glory. In liberal Protestantism, on the other hand, there has long been an awareness that the premises of the Augustinian theodicy—

Original Sin and the Fall, divine transcendence and the "unreality" of evil—are deeply dissonant in the modern mind. In response, liberalism took the opposite tack of relocating surd evil within God's own being—producing a mildly startling distinction between God's good intentions and his ability to perform. Professor E. S. Brightman was probably the most thoughtful exponent of this position,[4] which turned on a sharp disjunction: either divine sovereignty or the divine goodness. Between these two, his choice was clear, and so perhaps it would be for most of us, if it comes to *that* choice.

Further toward the fringe of liberalism there was a variety of efforts to salvage God's goodness—or at least to firm up the ground under human values—by shifting the chief agency for good and evil over onto the human side. Here the hope was raised that natural evil can be largely mastered by science and technology, and no great alarm over the fact that the same technology that conquers natural hazards keeps on generating new threats to human well-being. There was, when I was young, considerable encouragement in the brave thought that not even God could make a Stradivarius without Antonio, but that was before its converse could have been conceived, that not even God could have made an Auschwitz without a Hitler. And I still recall my vivid sense of topsy-turvy when I came upon a poem, on a student assembly bulletin board back in the 'thirties, that told of the conversion of an erstwhile disbeliever. He had supposed that neither he nor God had any real need of each other, but the sight of

4. Edgar Sheffield Brightman, *The Problem of God* (New York: The Abingdon Press, 1930).

Christ on his Cross had brought home the truth that God's cause in this world is in mortal danger and desperately needs men to save it. The unforgettable punch line:

Courage, God, I come!

I am very much aware that these comments on the gropings of Christians and others for answers to the inescapable perplexities of good and evil—for there is "the problem of the *good*" as well as evil!—do not amount to a complete or even coherent survey of the enterprise. Nor is there time and space here for a fully developed theodicy, even if I had one to offer. Happily, however, I can in good conscience urge both Farrer and Hick upon the reader—and Hick if he insists upon a single choice. For my purposes here, a sort of homily must suffice—a sermon that begins with an amateur's reading of the problem in Scripture and that concludes with what I hope is an honest and relevant "application" of the biblical wisdom about "overcoming evil with good" as Christians have tested this in the course of life and in the face of death.

For it strikes me forcibly that the biblical people come at this whole issue of God's presence in the world's torments in a different temper than one sees in the standard theodicies, especially those in the Augustinian succession. Scripture has no misgivings anywhere about God's freedom and omnicompetence. Everywhere, his aboriginality, his divine initiative and resourcefulness and sole deity stand secure against an encompassing polytheism and the chronic defections of his wayward Covenant People. Nobody in the Bible supposes that God's own fate is locked into the fortunes of his creation and it is unthinkable that anything creaturely can finally defeat his purposes. His final goal—the rule of righteousness and the reign of love—is never hedged or sold short. What is more, the theme of God's self-possession is as clear in the "mythological" passages as elsewhere—which is decidedly not the case in the Greek and Oriental mythologies.

It is, therefore, all the more remarkable that what these biblical people are really interested in is God's hazardous involvement in history—tragic and heart-rending as this has been made by man's defiance and his self-stultifying attempts to repudiate God's sovereignty and grace. Genesis gives the classic statement of the theme. God begins the creation as a deliberate venture in developing a community of finitely free creatures capable of blessedness and of sharing in his infinite love. There is an astute commentary on the risks of this venture in one of Thomas Mann's most brilliant chapters ("Prelude in Egypt") where he reports the angelic dissatisfactions with God's enthusiasm for creating *men* when he could have "let matters rest once and for all at [*their*] decent and honorable existence."

> Out of sheer restlessness and lack of exercise; out of the purest "much wants more"; out of a capricious craving to see, after the angel and the brute, what a combination of the two would be like; out of all these motives, and impelled by them [God] entangled himself in folly and created a being notoriously unstable and embarrassing. And then, precisely because it was such an undeniable miscreation, he set his heart upon it in magnificent self-will and made such a point of the thing that all heaven was offended.
>
> . . . With this being, then—in other words, man

> —evil came into the world. . . . Through the creation of the finite life-and-death world of form no least violence was done to the dignity, spirituality, majesty or absoluteness of a God who existed before and beyond the world. And thus up to now one could not speak seriously of error in any full or actual sense of the word. It was different with the ideas, plans and desires which were now supposed to be up in the air, the subject of confidential conversations with Shemmael [viz., the covenant with a Chosen People, etc.].[5]

It was, then, God's free choice to produce an enterprise one part of which would be under the reflex control of divine *fiat* (natural order) and the other (angels and men) with a narrow range of real freedom. In retrospect, it looks like an experiment in which the odds were stacked against success. Adam's chances for preserving his innocence and bliss seem now pathetic. But what was the alternative? Some sort of moral automaton? And would that have been really better, in the long run?[6] We cannot know, of course. What we do know is that the Eden story tells of a God who is undeniably "in charge" but who is also bilked and baulked by his own custom-crafted creatures—and this on either the Irenaean surmise that the first man was created immature so that he could grow up (to

5. Thomas Mann, *Joseph the Provider* (New York: Alfred A. Knopf, 1944), pp. 4–5, 9.

6. Cf. Hick, *op. cit.*, pp. 301–11, for an interesting "demonstration" that it is *logically inconceivable* that God could "have so constituted men that they could be guaranteed freely to respond to Himself in authentic faith and love and worship"—because that would have involved the abridgement of human freedom. Hick's analogy for this, following Antony Flew, is the unfree relationship of a hypnotized person to his hypnotist.

"learn by doing"), or on the Augustinian hypothesis of an originally perfect creature who came a fearful cropper over that forbidden fruit

> . . . whose mortal taste
> Brought death into the world, and all its woes.

This shaky start is then followed, throughout the rest of the Old Testament, by a series of misadventures in which the Almighty is forever having to improvise in response to some new human waywardness and to fall back on Plans B or C. The history of Israel is a very strange story, by any mythological or metaphysical canon you choose: God and man in protracted moral struggle, with no doubt about God's freedom and grace, and yet with almost nothing coming off according to the program. The Chosen People promptly misunderstood their unique role in human history—and the "unchosen" peoples were visibly unimpressed by God's provision for their salvation through Israel. This becomes the burden of the prophets and apocalyptists: God's warfare against unrighteousness and inhumanity; his promise and provision for his knowledge and love "to cover the earth as the waters cover the sea" (cf. Hab. 2:14). Job can raise the doubt, in reverent anguish, that God is just; he can, in high religious conscience, reject the pious bromides of his false comforters—and he can be silenced by a show of force that scarcely amounts to persuasion.

The same pattern continues when we shift to the New Testament. The mission of the Messiah-come-in-the-flesh has one announced aim ("the lost sheep of the house of Israel" [Matt. 10:6; 15:24]) and yet another actual outcome ("Lo, we turn to the Gentiles" [Acts 13:46]). The history of the Christian church begins with illusory hopes of an imminent *Parousia.* And then, after that first miscalculation, it has continued for nearly two millennia with perennial crises and transvaluations of its original mission and message.

These biblical stories are a mirror held up to the human condition. But, whereas in pagan mythology and philosophy, this picture of God in the Bible would imply a degradation of his being and glory, in the biblical mind these signs of man's partially successful resistance to God's designs serve to illuminate the axis-theme of biblical theology: God's freedom *and* his forbearance, his unmerited mercy *and* his omnicompetence (as contrasted with omnipotence). In this view, God's unswerving pursuit of his goals for man in the midst of the turmoils of human history is an even more striking proof of his providence and total investment than any form of aloofness could ever be. For there is never any question as to who has the initiative in nature and history or where the final power lies. The possibilities of history and the provisions for the mystery of salvation are what they are by the elect counsel and design of the Most High, beside whom there is no other. God reveals his moral expectations (Torah) to men, he pronounces judgment on their deviations, he visits his wrath on the rebels—and all this is talked about in language that is frankly anthropomorphic because it is also apophatic. But the purpose of it all is not the juridical imposition of Torah nor the condign punishment of offenders but rather the gathering of faithful persons into a fully human community by the various means of moral suasion of which grace is the chief!

In biblical terms, God's maintenance of his freedom does not require ontic barriers for his self-defense. Because he really is sovereign, he truly is free to allow evil as the dark shadow of corrupted good and yet sovereign to veto its final triumph. The sovereignty that reigns unchallenged is not as absolute as the sovereignty that accepts the risks of involvement and yet also provides appropriate resources for human fulfillment even in the depths of tragedy. If this sort of reflection strikes you as a diminution of God's Almighty Power, that, too, is a sign of our ironic situation: i.e. that Christian theodicy has come to rely almost exclusively on notions of immutability and impassibility which were, originally, only hermeneutic aids for interpreting the biblical testimony about a desperately involved God in terms quite different from any of the then reigning polytheisms.

But surely it should be decisive that this biblical witness is summed up in the life and teaching of Jesus Christ—and in his death, resurrection, and triumph. There the problem of evil and God's goodness stands forth in its starkest form—and is answered in a way designed to provide the Christian with his liveliest hope in life and death. The Incarnation is the recapitulation, in a single human life in a specific historical episode, of the entire enterprise of God's judgment, mercy, and sovereign grace in all lives, all times, all circumstances. It is, as you know, a formal and substantial heresy (maintained, however, by many who suppose themselves "orthodox") to interpret Christ's passion and death as a merely human event that left the God-Father unaffected. The Christian tradition understands the Cross in far more scandalous terms:

O Love divine! what has Thou done?
The immortal God hath died for me!
The Father's co-eternal Son
Bore all my sins upon the tree;
The immortal God for me hath died!
My Lord, my Love is crucified.

Here is a traditional version of the "death of God" (dated 1742)—as orthodox as the Definition of Chalcedon.

There is, therefore, no warrant in the Gospel stories for a picture of God as immune from the assaults on love and dignity that are staples of ordinary life. Freely and for love of us all the God-Father sent his only Son into the world—into our history and its tragedies—to expose himself to every stage and sort of human weakness and privation. The point stressed most in the birth-narratives is not the glory of the miracles but the indignity and squalor of the historical circumstances. Moreover, the rest of the Gospels' account is shaped around Christ's sufferance of the powers of evil—out of all due proportion for proper "biographies." Their motive for this is the fact that here is their prime test-case for the whole idea of God's provident presence in the deepest slough of man's despond.

God sends his Messiah to the lost sheep of the house of Israel and they reject his claims—but only as prototypes of all others who will ever thereafter reject them. As an unauthorized rabbi, Jesus distills the quintessence of the Law and the Prophets, only to have it go unheeded by those whose highest concern was the very same righteousness of that Law he was transvaluing for them and for all mankind. His frustration at being ignored by those he sought to serve drove him to tears on the Mount of Olives, to outrage in the Temple. The stories of "Passion Week" are focused on his desolation at the end: Gethsemane, Pilate's tribune, the Via Dolorosa, Golgotha. The nadir of it all is the cry of dereliction matched with a final word of utter trust: "Father, into your hands I commit my spirit."

One need not risk the heresy of patripassianism in order to take all this with profound seriousness. Sabellius' error lay in his confusions of the distinctive "offices and ministries" of the "persons" of the Trinity. But the live nerve of the truth he exposed—and mis-stated—runs through every valid Christology (and theodicy, since the two are finally the same). There *is* a cross in the heart of God. The Provident Mystery is involved in the agony of sin *with us*. It matters more for the triumph of righteousness that grace be finally invincible than that it should ever be irresistible.

Nor does this theme of strength made perfect in weakness end with the resurrection. Pentecost was a brave beginning for the church but her first centuries are a curious compound of pathos and glory. The first Christians were an insignificant minority, even in Judaism, with sadly mistaken hopes for their future here on earth. The second generation was expelled from the original Jewish matrix and yet also rejected by the Gentiles, accused by the Romans of misanthropy and atheism. The subsequent history of the church poses the same question in each of the successive crises that she has weathered: how on earth has she survived? No adequate answer seems possible without some reference to some notion of providence.

It is, therefore, an urgent question for contemporary theology as to whether we can replace the traditional theodicies based on God's transcendence with some version of the "theology of the cross" (*theologia crucis*) that yokes Christ's cross with ours. In defense of the divine sovereignty, traditional theology opted for a view of God that lifted him above the malignancies of sin and evil. But this carried one of two implications: either he was above the battle or, if he but passed the word, the world's woes and weeping would vanish. When it was complained that this was not the highest goodness men could conceive (and therefore unworthy of God), the answer was given that God's counsels are inscrutable and his ways past finding out. This brazen begging of the question served to quiet the doubts of some of the faithful but it left the rest with John Stuart Mill's blunt disjunction: if God is able to prevent evil and does not, he is not good; if he would prevent evil and cannot, he is not almighty. Many a sensitive Christian has writhed on the horns of this dilemma, since neither alternative is compatible with the essence of his faith.

Meanwhile, the new paganism, from Voltaire to Sartre, has found the courage or despair to reject the whole scheme *in toto*. Theodicy, in any of its classical forms (Greek or Christian), turns on the prior assumption that being and goodness are correlative, that the matrix of existence is orderly and that evil is, literally, the *ab-surdum*. But there is simply no problem if the matrix itself is absurd and if the only order, freedom, and values are those supplied by human episodes of rational freedom in a context of encompassing unreason. For Heidegger, the untowardness of existence (to which, as a Nazi, he contributed) proves the absence of God. Sartre turned up nauseated from squinting at the surds of existence until he could integrate them in a total ontology of absurdity. What should be noted is that the moral effect of this new paganism is the same as that of the immutability-impassibility doctrines. In both, man is left alone with both his grandeurs and his miseries.

The impassibility doctrines come in two styles: with and without pity. The upholders of sheer sovereign power are led by their pitiless logic to one or another hypothesis about the predetermined damnation of the vast mass of mankind—in whose eternal perdition God's glory shines forth untarnished. For those more tenderhearted, there are the universalist alternatives, which work from the same premise of divine transcendence but with a contrary projection of "last things." Neither of these options is satisfactory for they both decline the risks of "God with us" here in the heart of darkness.

There is yet another complication in the problem of evil in our time. It comes from a steadily decreasing tolerance of human misery by modern men whose hopes have been raised to the level of real confidence that misery can be reduced or banished. Parlous as it is, the human lot today, speaking generally and comparatively, is ampler and more open to improvement than in any age since Eden. And yet far more of us are far more discontented with *our* lot than any generation ever was. Our progress in overcoming the tyrannies of nature—easing pain, enhancing health, postponing death, multiplying creature comforts—has formed a new mind-set that has no precedent in human history: misery is less to be endured than overcome, and man has the means within his grasp to overcome it. What once men suffered mutely as inevitable they now demand relief from because they are convinced it is possible. Markham's "man with the hoe" has become McLuhan's man with TV hypnosis.

But the millennium still awaits and men are still denied the full harvest of the secular apocalypse as advertised. Hunger is still a torment in the world where, we are told, there are ample technical resources to wipe it out. Populations go on exploding in spite of the fact that there are available means for rational family planning. Poverty persists in sight of affluence, the human community disintegrates despite instant (and constant!) communication. Freedom has brought us headaches along with hallelujahs.

And this has generated an imperious mood of aggrieved innocence in modern man—a rising impatience amongst those whose reach has exceeded their grasp (which must surely be most of us). The old pagans blamed their misfortunes on the gods. Our Christian forefathers tended to blame their indignities on nature—and themselves (original sin). It would not now occur to many of us to accuse nature; still fewer are inclined to blame ourselves. "Guilt" is recessive: parents are to blame for their children's alienations, "society" is the scapegoat for the parents, and so it goes. We used to speak of "anxiety *and* guilt"; there was an Age of Anxiety of which W. H. Auden was celebrant. Now the conventional sense of guilt is gone, or going, and in its place resentment runs unchecked. The Age of Anxiety has turned into the Age of Outrage with Dylan Thomas for a bard.

> Do not go gentle into that goodnight;
> Rage, rage against the dying of the light.

The bitter fruit of all this is a temper of self-righteousness and mutual recrimination that leaves the problem of moral evil and human tragedy less intelligible than ever, and that makes its practical solution quite impossible. If others are to blame for our condition, or for the human condition, then let them rectify it. The part of the offended is to demand that rectification. This temper of injured innocence has gone far to poison intergroup and international relations everywhere.

It may, therefore, be unfashionable but urgent to reconsider the intentions of two traditional doctrines that once shaped the Christian perception of mankind's corporate responsibility for his human woes: original sin and total depravity. Allowing for, and rejecting, the misanthropic excesses to which these notions are susceptible, let us notice their two interdependent aims and functions. They were designed, in the first place, to undercut all claims of human self-righteousness and merit—and so to establish our radical need of God's sheer unmerited favor as the single source of any possible salvation. There are, it may be, other ways to do this. The essential point, however, is that without some such sense of need and dependence, the biblical meaning of faith and reconciliation is stultified. In the second place, the traditional doctrine of "fallen human nature" provided an etiology of moral evil; it "explained" man's misery in terms of his enmity to God and his correlative inhumanity to his neighbor—and himself. Thus, one might think, it would go with our modern accent on man's responsibility for human culture to hold him equally responsible for the spoliation of the good world in which he was set and for the miscarriage of the possibilities provided him for true community. It is high time, therefore, to take seriously the biblical testimony about God's involvement in the human lot made miserable by man's rebellion and to seek a richer understanding of the apostolic faith that, since God *is* love, the essence of his providence is *com*passion.

In such a search we are, of course, stuck with the prime article of Christian belief: that the Maker of heaven and earth wrought well and that the creation even as it stands is a more appropriate matrix for God's Kingdom than any other alternative. From this it follows that if human freedom and love abused are the chief agencies in the ruination of the human enterprise, then freedom and love rightly used must indeed be values of such ultimate concern that God Almighty deliberately risked a creation like this to make them possible. In this sense, it *is* the best of all possible worlds, *for what God had in mind.* In his forbearance of the havoc wrought by freedom and love abused, his ways *are* past finding out—unless there is some hope of the entire venture ever being seen steadily and whole. All the alternatives—save atheism—are blasphemous: that he could have done better and didn't, that he tried and failed, that love and hate are equally ultimate, that the God who does not "intervene" also couldn't care less. Better atheism than any of these. The atheist, of course, has a different problem. Given the human abuse of freedom (or any other etiology of misery) what is *his* ground for any hope at all that such men can rightwise their own existence and achieve their true possibilities within *his* terms of reference? Here, obviously, the burden of overbelief shifts to the other side.

The Christian hope springs from the faith that the providence of the *possibilities and potencies* in this creation is sufficient for the triumph of God's good purposes in the optimum realization of human blessedness. In this sense, what God made and goes on making is *good;* even in its corruption, the residues of created good remain. It would then follow that the miscarriages of some of these good possibilities are the shadow side of the possibility for the realizations of others. Our misery is an ironic testimony to the fact of our awareness that blessedness is the goal for which human existence was originally designed. And if the question arises as to whether God was just or wise in making us free if being free would make us miserable, we then stand on the threshold of the biblical insight that God's "justice" is not so much a matter of his enforcing the law as of his insisting on our freedom—and of his reconciling us even in our offenses against the law by grace *alone* (i.e. freely and for love). This is the gist of the classical doctrine of "justification." Having made us free, and also liable to abuse that freedom, God engages himself in the hazards of our invested freedom—and so provides the way for freedom, abused, to be converted to its proper use for our good and his glory.

The Christian Gospel is the good news that in this world just as it is, and in our lives just as they are, the possibility of God's righteous rule in our hearts and lives is always a live option (". . . and Jesus came preaching, the

Kingdom of God is *at hand*" [cf. Matt. 4:17, 10:7; Mark 1:15]). This is what the world is for: to be the arena in which God's righteousness becomes man's blessedness. This is what our lives are for: to receive the Kingdom through Christ its bearer and to share with him the love of the father in the Holy Spirit. This is

> the secret hidden for long ages and through many generations, but now disclosed to God's people, to whom it was his will to make it known—to make known how rich and glorious is his grace among all nations. The secret is this: Christ in your midst, the hope of glory! [Col. 1:26–27, NEB]

To know this is to know that our lives are in his hands and that he is in the thick of history with us, providing the potentials of meaningful experience and yet refusing either to coerce or to bless us without our own participation. Here he is in our existence—working, suffering, loving, enduring the indignities of our rebellion and sin as we do—not because he is weak but because he is loving, not because he needs our aid to help him win but because our lives require a climate of divine compassion in order to come to their flower and fruit. Love is redemptive only when it is intimate enough to be personal, unselfish enough to be truly trustworthy. The Passion of Christ did *not* end at Golgotha: it goes on and on to the end of the world, wherever the passions of men go unredeemed. The sacrifice of Calvary is endlessly efficacious, not as a substitute for the sacrifices to which love calls us, but as a purgation of our sacrificial love from self-pity and bitterness. God-with-us: in life's turmoils and drudgery, its vigils and sunbursts, unravelling and reweaving the strands of our memories and hopes, judging, thwarting, leaving us to suffer for our own misdeeds and those of others and yet never forsaking us even in our sufferings. God-with-us: not to dominate but to bless and yet also to prevent the *final* triumph of our resistance to his righteous rule. God-with-us: endlessly patient, endlessly concerned, endlessly resourceful. Here in the biblical secret of Immanuel, the Provident Mystery of God is "present" in the very same projects to which he has assigned us, concerned above all that our experiences come to their created potential. This, or something like it, is faith's answer to the problem of evil.

Even so, the test of such a conviction comes only in the cumulative experience of trustful living—of having our trials and tribulations recognized as the temperings of faith, of being exposed to the strains and torque of the moral conflict in which love is offered and repudiated or corrupted but not withdrawn, of plumbing the heights and depths of joy and sorrow, rejoicing and mourning, glowing health and searing pain, holy and unholy living, the fear of death and the hope of holy dying. These are the "proofs" of God's providence that come finally to be believed and trusted.

What cannot be borne by any man aware of his human dignity—and the dignity of others—is meaningless, wasted, useless life. What we cannot endure is the fear that evil has the final word at life's end. A world in which senseless disasters and catastrophes occur all too often can still be lived in, courageously and grace-fully, *if* the lives affected can be seen, or can be believed, to have finally significant meaning, here and hereafter. Meaningless pain or active cruelty are simply outrageous and destructive of morally meaningful faith. But pain that comes with fruitful travail or useful service may not only be borne but be ennobling. Illness can crumple our morale, or it can be lived with in the light of the instrumental value we attach to health as an agency of our humanity. Heroism is mostly a matter of a man caring more greatly for something other than himself—or caring for himself as the servant of some other value that ranks higher on his scale than his own self-interest.

As a man learns to live in such a spirit—if only fitfully and imperfectly—he comes more and more to appreciate and reach out for the communion of those who have found life good and are devoted to making it good for others, he gains more and more compassion for those whose painful struggles or sodden apathy are equally unavailing. In such an odyssey, God's presence is our ward against loneliness, lostness, and that immoderate love of what has been that dulls our taste for what more there is to come that we may share in. Life becomes more grace-filled and thus more graceful—and the confidence of our trust confirmed and strengthened. And all this, mind you, springs from a "theology of the Cross"!

For those whose lives have begun to be hid with God in Christ, the query about evil gets to be less urgent than what the good is in the situation at hand—and how the provident presence of grace opens up new futures with new meanings that can redeem the bitter residues of past estrangements. The ground for our belief that the battle is worth our best is not that God is above it calling the shots, but that he is *in* it sharing the blows—*and that he is going to win it*, for us men and for our salvation! *Christus Victor* is not our fairy godmother—nor the immutable, impassible Absolute whose relations with creation are non-reciprocal. He is, rather, the author of our salvation, the pioneer of God's providence for our destiny, the power of love that reconciles.[7]

The genius of Christian faith is the learning by living that evil, both physical and moral, is bad (and to be avoided and resisted) but that evil is not invincible and we can reject its claim to have the final word in our lives and others. The solid core of all damnation is the false persuasion that we are done for, that the powers of sin and death have no match, that despair is an honest reading of existence. What we need to know is that all of the power wielded by "the powers of sin and death" is actually supplied *by us* in our sin, pride, and fear, as we feed the lie that evil has the upper hand.

It is our Christian calling to fight against all the ills and woes that afflict mankind and against their human causes and provocations. To leave misery unalleviated, to leave social revolution to the angry and selfish, to stand aloof from the agonies of the new world a-borning is to make it all too plain that we are not interested in the compassion of God but only in our own passive hope of his impassible providence. The unanimous "answer" by the saints and heroes of the faith to the problem of evil is disconcertingly simple: evil is overcome by the intelligent, competent concern of people willing to pay the price of conflict. This seems the wrong answer for those of us who think we could devise a better world where all was joy and bliss.

7. Cf. Col. 1:19–27.

But there it is—and its truth can only be verified by the ventures of that Christian gallantry that does not seek pain but rather undertakes to reduce it, that labors with no guidelines save need and opportunity, that does not have to foresee the distant scene in order to know where the action is here and now.

The chorus of these lectures, repeated after every verse, is that God's providence is his provident presence in all the exigencies of creation. This is never more meaningful than his presence in the anguish of guilt and self-reproach. Here, his grace is to be seen in his pro-vision for the efficacy of repentance and pardon, on the one hand, and for the strength of comfort and hope, on the other. Repentance is neither grovelling nor flip remorse; it is the honest recognition of one's own capacity for sin and one's utter need of grace to bear the consequences of sin and to fend off temptation. Pardon is neither a cancelling of the past nor the condonation of evil, but the affirmation of love where wrath was expected and a newly opened future where guilt had foreseen only punishment.

By the same token, "comfort" is not an easement of the demands for righteousness nor a smoothing of the upward way. *Con-fortare* means to offer strength by *standing beside* someone in need of strength. God does not leave us to go it alone, but then neither does he carry any but "the *young* lambs in his bosom." He summons the rest of us to stand on our own feet, to take responsibility for our freedom and its entail—assuring us of needful strength that comes from his standing with and for us. Hope is not the projection of our wishes onto the calendar of the forthcoming future. It is, rather, the confidence that God is holding that future open so that its potential for meaningful participation will remain, so that life will still be fit for living and dying, secure in God's provident presence in life and death and destiny.

V

Providence and the Christian Style of Life

The strength of the disbelievers' cause comes mainly from their undeniable commitment to human values and the incompatibility, in their minds, between authentic humanism and traditional Christianity. The implied contrast is reflected in current rhetorical fashion. The word "secular" is newly favored; its synonyms are all triumphant: "modern," "free," "mature," "autonomous." Its antonym, "ecclesiastical," is sadly tarnished, with cognates that are all pejorative: "static," "other-worldly," "credulous," "irrelevant." The world and modern men have "come-of-age," so runs the oft-repeated slogan. They have grown out of the perpetual immaturity to which traditional Christianity had condemned them; they have cut the leading strings of religion. Man is finally on his own, his future open and hopeful. "Mankind," said Voltaire, "will not be truly free and happy until the last king is throttled with a noose made from the entrails of the last priest." It has not yet come to that, but near enough. The vast majority of mankind are no longer controlled or even strongly influenced by their religious institutions. Jargon phrases like "the end of Christendom," "the end of the Christian era," "the end of Europe," are popular and symptomatic even though misleading. What they reflect is the long tradition of reproach against traditional Christianity that it was "modern" man's chief obstacle to self-realization. The Calvinists burnt Servetus; the Catholics burnt Bruno; the Protestants drove modern philosophy and science beyond the pale of orthodoxy; the Catholics reprobated modernity (as in the *Syllabus of Errors*) and withdrew into an authoritarian enclave (until Vatican II). From Rousseau to Altizer, traditional Christianity has been a broadside target for both rebels and reformers. But what now, when the erstwhile dominance of Christianity (always vastly overrated) has been so nearly broken in those areas where it once was strong? If the world has come of age and if this means man's emancipation from priestcraft and superstition, from bigotry and moralism and organized hypocrisy (the main items in the radicals' indictment) then these are indeed days of rejoicing. We will, no doubt, run out of kings to garrotte before the supply of clerics is exhausted, but even the clerical threat to human happiness is fading fast and can easily be contained.

The point at issue in this double reversal is the nature of *true* "humanism." Christianity began with the promise of "the more abundant life," in conscious challenge to the impoverished dignity and prospect of life in what was then the "modern" world. Down through the centuries, the claim that Christianity is the true champion of humanity has been repeated by the doctors of the church—and partially realized, too, in ways now conveniently forgotten.

The humanizing influences of Christianity in the ancient world were actually quite extraordinary.

The truth is that the ruling notion of Christian social ethics since the days of Constantine (when the church had the responsibility for this *saeculum* thrust upon it) has been *a universal human community in this world*, in which love, reason, and religion would overarch and temper the residuary chaos which is the "normal" drift of human politics. This was the moral essence of the church's campaigns for a universal language and liturgy, for a universal civil and canon law, for a *philosophia perennis*, for a supranational organization. The very notion of "humanity" as a concrete social universal, inclusive of *all* nations, races tongues, and classes—and both sexes!—owes more to Christianity (traditional Christianity, at that!) than to any other source. The modern meanings of words like "freedom," "brotherhood," "neighbor," "equality," "justice," "human rights," etc., are demonstrably derivative from Christian sources.

What happened, of course, was that Christianity never came even close to realizing its vision of the Kingdom of God on earth and, instead, began to corrupt it. What needs to be noticed, however, is that the most powerful stimuli to corruption came from the incessant pressures of the secular society that the church was unable, or unwilling, to resist. The constant policy of every major European monarch from Constantine to Franco has been a church subservient to imperial or national politics. One can speak of the Middle Ages as an "age of faith" only if one remembers that it never achieved much more than a slight amelioration of the organized inhumanity of the feudal system. The struggles between the popes and the princes of medieval Europe ended in the *cuius regio, eius religio* ("the ruler decides the religion", easily the baldest formula for secularism ever proposed) at the "Religious Peace" of Augsburg (1555). Protestantism has never been able really to dominate the social ethos of any large population for more than a generation or so. One can speak, but only with drastic qualifications, of "Catholic Spain," or Portugal or Ireland (but not of France or Italy). "Holy Russia" was always more a motto than a description. This is why all the talk about the "post-Christian era" is significant on other grounds than its historical accuracy. What it does is to remind us of how Christianity once got both the credit and the blame for a great deal she only endured or connived at—or, occasionally, tried valiantly to reform. Now she gets only the blame.

Over a long, and consistently ambiguous, course and partly in the interest of survival, the church fell in with the political concerns of its environment and became, in effect, yet another rival to the secular powers for secular power. There is a theocratic bent in Christianity that tends to identify the visible church with the invisible Kingdom and this had led to frequent ventures in "establishment" and various bids for political advantage that sometimes saved the institution from impotence but rarely served her prophetic vision of the Christian commonwealth. The church's willing alliance with repressive secular power-structures, her use of the "power of the keys" in the suppression of human freedom, her pathological immobilism in times of revolution—and all of these as rampant in classical Protestantism as in Catholicism—had two tragic results. First, they failed to achieve their goals and, second, they gave the church a bad name. Christianity never closed the gap between its promises and performance.

Thus, when the modern age began to emerge—aided *and* resisted in every major aspect by churchmen!—there was Christianity ready to hand as the obvious scapegoat for the resentments and frustrations of men impatient for emancipation. They had forgotten their hideously barbaric past; they did not realize how thin the veneer of Christian morality and manners had always been. They only knew that the human lot in their societies was unendurable and that the church was the avowed champion of the *status quo*. Marx took it for granted that religion and reaction were mutually interdependent; Blake hated Christianity because he blamed the English Establishment for throttling democracy; Freud was speaking to a consensus of the intelligentsia when he credited Christianity with a degrading influence on Western man's self-estimate; Sartre was trading on a massive bias when he claimed that his brand of existentialism was truly humanistic. Nobody in this tradition has ever given a second thought to Jacques Maritain's counter-claim that Christianity is, and always has been, "the *true* humanism." [1]

Liberal Christianity was especially sensitive to the Enlightenment criticism and sought to blunt it by reasserting the prophetic tradition in the Bible and in historic Christianity. From Ritschl to Rauschenbusch and Reinhold Niebuhr, the "Social Gospel" sought to serve society as a

1. Sigmund Freud, *Civilization and Its Discontents*, translated by Joan Riviera (London: The Hogarth Press, Ltd., 1957), p. 45. Jacques Maritain, *True Humanism* (London: Geoffrey Bles, The Centenary Press, 1938).

social conscience and to come to grips with the appalling problems of human misery created by "moral men and immoral society"—a phrase that Niebuhr made familiar. G. B. Smith and Shailer Mathews preached the gospel for the secular city before Harvey Cox was born. The "Social Creed of the Churches" and the cognate pronouncements of the various churches and councils of churches have had a more powerful effect than most of us realize in forming the humanitarian conscience that now has come to energize the moral fervor of men who have discarded its Christian premises.

But the stigma remains. Even liberal Christianity fell short of what modernity was demanding: radical autonomy. It was not enough to blame Christianity for its ineffective efforts to lead the revolution. In a world come of age, it was the supernatural itself that had to go. Hence the demands for "religionless Christianity," for new strictures on "God-talk." Hence the general scorn for the parish-church as an agency of effective service, and the shattered morale of the parish clergy. Hence the onslaughts on the bad consciences of conventional Christians who feel guilty about the church's failures and yet also helpless to set things right.

Meanwhile, the rise and progress of man's new-found self-confidence has been steady and impressive. From Lord Herbert of Cherbury to Hobbes and the Deists, to Hume and the French revolutionaries, to Fichte and Feuerbach, to Marx, Mazzini and Nietzsche, to Freud and Heidegger and Sartre, a new sensibility has been growing in the Western world that is wholly preoccupied with the human situation and its inherent possibilities. Allied as it has been (albeit accidentally) with the concurrent rise and progress of modern science, invention, and technology, human self-confidence has moved from triumph to triumph over divine-right theories of throne and altar and their psycho-sociological progeny: religious credulity, "clericalism," and the exploitation of the undefended. The most impressive aspect of this complex development has been the steady growth of science and technology—which goes on flourishing in war and peace, with an Olympian indifference to the fact that it serves irreconcilable ideologies with an even-handed neutrality. It is in the development of technology that we can point to real progress, to splendid promises actually kept. But as for modernity's hopes for a brave new world of human happiness, these have had to be nourished rather more by hope than by achievement—which is to say, "modern" man has had to learn to live by one or another version of a *secular eschatology*!

Secular humanism has gotten much of its drive and self-assurance from the lure of utopia. This was clearly the case in the American and French revolutions, in the liberal ideologies of the nineteenth century, in the liberation of Latin America, in the Italian *Risorgimento*, in the Russian revolution and its spin-offs, in the rise of "the third world," in the Negro rebellion here at home. And every one of these bids for human freedom and dignity has been strongly animated by vivid hopes of the triumph of humanity in their victories. But the fact that all of these eschatological hopes have been aborted or denied—and not any longer by ecclesiastical villainy!—has finally begun to create a new crisis of confidence. What now for man in this new world *he* has called into being?

The positive goal of modern disbelief has always been human autonomy. Now that goal is either in hand or at hand. Christianity as a political establishment has lost or renounced its hegemony everywhere. Institutional religion continues as a minor factor of varying significance in national and international affairs but is nowhere dominant. From the Elbe to Dairen, from Murmansk to the Caspian, a militant humanism is in uncontestable control. The ruling spirit of European and American culture is secularist —and has been since the catastrophe of World War I and its aftermath. In America the secular principle was written into our Constitution and is one of the few items of consensus in our national self-consciousness. In the "third world," secularism was the only viable option from the beginning. By any definition a sociologist or historian could use, the consequence of the world "come-of-age" has been the displacement of all previous traditions of theonomy with one or another version of autonomy.

But it is almost as if the prospects of victory are more enchanting than its aftermath. As long as secularism was a protest against the manifest failures of Christianity to deliver on its promises for the human enterprise, it had a vital role, essentially corrective. Now, as a regnant ideology, its sufficiency is subject to the same stern questions that Christianity has been pelted with—and the preliminary "findings" have not been reassuring. There is a rueful irony in the fact that just as modern man's bid for autonomy is being allowed, a drastic disenchantment with the marvels of modernity begins to deepen and spread.

To begin with, there is the strife of systems and the chaos of ideologies. On the one side, there are the glaring faults in the democratic societies and the capitalistic systems, and these are fiercely prophesied against almost everywhere. On the other side and at the same time, there are the fading eschatological visions of the communist world. The Chinese are right about the Russians—they *are* "revisionists," and so is every communist ideology in the world that has survived its first generation. The revolution of rising expectations of what man on his own could make of the human lot—with science and technology as its servants—has raised hopes that, unfulfilled, have generated disillusionments that, in their turn, have driven revolutionaries from autonomy to anarchy to anomie—or to military dictatorship. In the secular eschatology, there is the vision of men becoming responsible as they become free, rational as they grow past credulity, co-operative as they gather into their growing cities, humane as the responsibility for health, education, and welfare is accepted and shared by the whole community. And only a misanthrope would murmur at such visions of free men in dynamic community—rational, co-operative, humane.

But the vision gets harder to be confident of. Its prophets are having to walk more and more by faith and less by sight. There is at least one common testimony in the mass media in which we live and move and have our being. It is this: more and more "modern" men have come to the conclusion that they have little or nothing to gain from rational, co-operative and humane behavior. What else does Vietnam mean, or Detroit or the Mid-East or Nigeria—or De Gaulle? And these are only symptoms of something deeper and more ominous that has been happening to the human spirit in our time: its radical alienation from any sort of *public environment*—"the objective world," "the common good," "universal human values," etc.—and the steady growth of a passionate autism. Modern literature (fiction, drama, poetry) and modern art (painting, sculpture, music) make this point and defend it. But then so also do the statistics of social anarchy and apathy—and so does the pall of anonymity and impersonality that blurs the faces of men who live in crowds that are not communities.

With a good deal of fervor, Freud denounced the pitiless, repressive forces of the "super-ego morality" of the *fin-de-siècle* ethos he knew and despised. And no good word has been said for the Puritan conscience in living memory. Most modern men said "good riddance" to their moralistic shackles with a lively hope that the resultant human situation would be infinitely superior—which is to say, more fully humane and more truly moral. Freud was as deeply concerned for a rational and honest morality as Kant ever was. But he also saw its obstacles, as Kant did not, in the stark conflict between the goals of personal development ("happiness") and the requirements of culture ("community") quite apart from the stultifications of religion.

> . . . It almost seems as if humanity could be most successfully united into one great whole if there were no need to trouble about *the happiness of individuals.*
>
> . . . So in every individual the two trends, one towards personal happiness and the other towards unity with the rest of mankind, must contend with each other; so must the two processes of individual

> and of cultural development oppose each other and dispute the ground against each other.[2]

And now, alas, what Freud feared most is what has happened: "modern" man, lover of humanity as he professes himself, has generally opted for happiness versus community and is in a grim way of forfeiting both.

A decade ago, Erich Kahler, one of the most perceptive of our contemporary analysts, surveyed the mutations in human self-consciousness in our time, as these have been reflected in modern art and existentialist philosophy—and his diagnosis remains essentially right even in a flux that makes most books ten years old seem hopelessly old-fashioned.[3] He points to "the emergence of a new sensibility" ("the experience of life as a simultaneity of the utterly diverse") and a concurrent new insensibility ("a new callousness required by modern atrocities and modern warfare").[4] He then traces these developments in a fascinating "documentary" of modern literature from Melville to Camus: the pervasive *malaise* of culture, the intensification of egoism, the subtilization of artistic techniques. His conclusion is brave and bleak:

> The luxuriant growth of the new sensibility has brought forth the most admirable artistic creations, which have enriched and deepened not only our life experience but the reality of our life itself. Yet the splendor of all these accomplishments should not blind us to the fact that they also carry a formidable danger. The arts, as well as science and technology,

2. Freud, *op. cit.*, pp. 135–36.
3. *The Tower and the Abyss: An Inquiry into the Transformation of the Individual* (New York: George Braziller, Inc., 1957).
4. *Ibid.*, pp. 135, 93.

> have enormously extended man's reach, but in the course of and through this very extension, they threaten to tear away the basis from which they sprang ["the unity and integrity of the human form," p. xiv]. They are about to destroy the human personality.[5]

It would be bigotry and bad history to suggest that these disenchantments with secular eschatology—they will get worse!—are heaven's retribution against human *hubris.* It would be more fitting for us to see in them heaven's judgment against Christianity's tragic failures to identify itself with the just aspirations of modern man for "happiness" *and* "community." *Ecrasez l'infâme* and "Burn, baby, burn" are both unfair and impolitic slogans, but the offenses that provoked them still lie at *our* door and must be repented of by real change or else we shall deserve the chaos they incite. Traditional Christianity did confound spiritual authority and "temporal sovereignty" (or political influence), dogma and the *consensus fidelium,* the Scripture and revelation, the magisterium and truth, servility and obedience, credulity and warranted belief. We are well shed of the shameless hypocrisies of conventional moralism publicly sanctioned by church and society and privately violated by churchmen and pillars of society. We would be as well shed of ecclesiastical institutions and ecclesiastics who confuse the preservation of the *status quo* with their service to the Kingdom.

But a litany of this sort returns us to the original question: who really *is* for man? What is likely to contribute most to the fullest realization of the human possibility? Is

5. *Ibid.,* p. 183.

it the secularist gospel of man on his own or the Christian faith in God's providence and man's radical dependence? The answer to these questions cannot be decided by fiat or referendum. For modern disbelief and the radical theologians the equation of God and man's immaturity is no longer open to critical re-examination. For the conservative and hyper-orthodox there is the reciprocal equation of disbelief and damnation. Neither will dislodge the other and, unfortunately, their mutual recriminations will shortly be drowned out by yet noisier breaches of the peace.

But it just may be that this unexpected impasse is itself a new "fullness of time" for the Christian mission in the modern world. Here is the chance and the demand for a newly self-conscious minority religion in the modern world to reformulate and press its original claims as a true humanism in the face of a regnant secularism newly uncertain of its prospects. Such claims would have to be rooted in two prime theses about the Christian style of life: first, that it is focused in this *saeculum* ("*this* world"), that it gains its buoyancy and gracefulness from its consciousness of God's provident presence in human existence—past, present, and future; and, second, that the true meanings of life are summed up in *death*, as the final "test" and triumph of providence. If such things were not so open to mindless ridicule nowadays, one might speak of Jeremy Taylor's "Rules of Holy Living *and* Holy Dying" or John Donne's "Death's Duel."

The Christian style of life was first fashioned and modelled by men who understood well enough that their witness to the truth, their conceptions of human community as a fabric of grace, and their indifference to the standing order, would make them unwelcome in the "modern" world of the Roman Empire. Their secret weapon, however, was not revolutionary violence, nor a hedonist withdrawal, nor a lofty and lugubrious pessimism. Actually, by comparison with Marcus Aurelius, St. Paul sounds downright debonair! Nor were the Christians "cockeyed optimists," as their attitudes toward martyrdom make plain. But what did help to spread the Christian cause was their evident consciousness of being freed from primal and ultimate anxieties—that was God's business! —and their liberation to live intensely in the present and hopefully toward the future with no expectation of ease and favor and no fear of finally counting for nothing.

The Christian style of life is built around a biblical realism that looks at life unblinking, that sees it for the castle perilous it really is, that reacts to its frustrations and dangers with a faith that lets honest fear teach men humility and compassion *in community*. The really "stylish" Christian takes it for granted that existence is tenuous and untoward—the nice guys do often finish last, if they aren't finished off first. But, oddly enough, he is seldom bitter and outraged that it should be so; he is not smothered with self-pity, not driven to strike out blindly against his tormentors. What's more, this cannot wholly be accounted for as what Nietzsche sneeringly called a slave mentality. The stylish Christian finds life *good—this* life in *this* world. And so he takes the bitter and the sweet with tears and laughter because he is so sure that this life and this world are all as fully and really in God's care and keeping as the affairs of the angels and saints in heaven. He sees his joys and sorrows in the perspective of life as a training ground for growing persons—all of it provided and cared for by grace. He is not "patient" with any misery that human wit and effort can prevent or allay—his own or others—but his courage and devotion do not fluctuate with the odds against his "success." He is, as Luther said, "the most free lord of all and subject to no one"—in this sense undominated by society and "the world"—and yet also he is "most bound by love and subject to every one." He is a man for others precisely because he is not a man on his own.

Such people—and they really do add up to an impressive cloud of witnesses—are neither apathetic nor insatiable. They can endure their actual fears because they are not afraid of the ultimate anxiety of cosmic loneliness. They do not have to fake their courage, or be compulsive about their dignity and prerogatives. They know that the summation of the final meaning of life is so far out of their hands that an interim clamor for autonomy is fatuous—but, by the same token, they also know that life *does* "mean intensely, and it means good."

But the life of grace that lives fully in the present is also life open to the future and to death. For all that life means now must really await judgment as to what it will have meant when it can all be seen in just perspective. For the Christian, this turns on his faith in God's providence for the human future as well as the past. Such a faith knows as well as any skeptic that our proximate futures are inscrutable and that our final future is, literally, inconceivable. But it does believe that God's providence for our freedom, identity and power to love will continue to "the end" as it has from "the beginning."

The root meaning of Christian eschatology is twofold. On the one hand, every "moment" is a man's "last"—the last I have any right to count on. Each one is a vital intersection of our time and God's eternity. Such moments, and days, should therefore be lived as if they were the *eschata* —which is to say: what matters is to make the most of each present "life-time." On the other hand, the truest meaning our lives will ever be known to have had, even when they are finally added up, has already been revealed in the life and death and victory of Jesus Christ. The divine providence for our future has already been previsioned in that one event in our human past on which all our human futures hinge and in which we are all included.

By now I have said, in as many different ways I can think of, that God's providence is not an interventive "cause" in history but rather his provision for and his valid assessment of the possibilities and actualizations of creation and of historical existence within the prospectus of creation. This is part of the meaning of the symbol of the Last Judgment—i.e. history finally set in its total retrospect. And this is why the acid test of any Christian's faith in providence is found in his *expectationes* of that summative event in every individual existence that makes all present moments past. No man's "hope for years to come" is better than interim unless his "expectation" of his future (including his death) has already been committed to God's love and tendance.

There is a tremendous line in the Niceo-Constantinopolitan Creed that is more often mumbled than declared and that gets bleached in our conventional English translation: ". . . and I look for the resurrection of the dead . . ." The verb in the Greek original, *prosdekomenon,* is a present participle; and its correct Latin translation is a present indicative, *exspecto* ("I *expect*!"). In both cases they mean, "I'm actually counting on the resurrection . . ." Only the morbid have ever meant by this that they wanted out of the secular city forthwith. But the "stylish" Christians have used it to match their awareness of death's certainty (*memento mori,* and all that!) with their confidence that life and death are both within God's providence.

Our guilty fears from the past, our anxious fears of the future, are all sublated in our fears of death. The fatal delusion in all utopias is that death does not rightly fit into their account of the human condition—for the more nearly ideal the human achievement, the more absurd its mortality. And so the human experience as a whole becomes finally absurd unless death has a summative meaning for our lives and destinies.

It goes with the flawed humanism of modern disbelief that there is a popular conspiracy to deny death's actuality or to cosmetize it, or else to react to it with outrage and incontinent grief. Even in Christian circles, you often get the doctrine of the *Phaedo,* that death is not really death but only the shuffling off its mortal coil by an immortal soul, off to join the choir invisible. We do not know how to die or what to die for—and so death is neither enemy nor friend but mostly a horror. And yet, in any large view of the human condition, life and death define each other.

The great patristic doctors (Athanasius, for example) realized that the worst blight on a man's will to live well was his fear of death. The force of this fear comes from our acceptance of its claim that it can naught *all* the values of life—that the best and the worst lie equal in the grave. And so the church developed one of its most interesting theories of man's salvation around the theme of *Christus Victor*—Christ's victory over the power of the demons to delude us into believing that their powers are ultimate. And this victory was won for us, on our ground, by one of our own kind, who suffered death's power only to have it broken by God's sovereign love. His disciples share in his victory in lively gratitude and in the offertory of their lives as their appropriate response to God's provident gifts of life and grace.

But the Christian style of life is not so much preoccupied with "the life of the world to come" as it is with the reflex significance of the Christian hope for life in and for this world. The chief New Testament passages that deal with death and resurrection are climaxed by comments on Christian morale here and now, in this life. After a long section on death and the Christian hope in his first letter to the Corinthian Christians—quite "modern" for the mid-first century!—St. Paul finally draws his "secular" conclusion:

> Therefore, brothers beloved, continue stedfast and secure, always abounding in the Lord's work [in *this* world!], knowing that whatever you do is never in vain, in the Lord. [I Cor. 15:58]

It belongs to the Christian style of life to confess God's providential responsibility for the ambiance of human existence and its meanings—creation, preservation, consummation. His faith in providence amounts to a confidence that God knows his business and is about it. The "demonstration" of this—sufficient for the hazards of faith—comes from our *memoriae* of what he has already done in the history of Incarnate Love, and in the pilgrim history of the people of God.

And yet it is of equal moment for any Christian humanism to confess that God has made us responsible for our share in human history, past and future. We were put on this earth to tend it, to turn it to the use and service of the human cause. This means careful stewardship of motherwit and reason, of life, time, and talents—all under the disciplines of love and community. Christian humanism is a summons, for God's sake and ours, to bring sanity and love and sacrificial service as oblations in the tasks of rescuing human life from indignity and in promoting the fullest achievement of the human possibility. Man is the maker of culture; he is also the corrupter of the cultures he makes. God provides for both, and holds his judgment firm against man's abuse of what would have been proper. He does not prevent man's inhumanity; he only vetoes its ever being vindicated as truly human. And this means, for all who live under such a providence, a high-hearted acceptance of their shares of both the world's work and its weeping.

If anything at all like this is true, it would really amount to an earnest affirmation of the human enterprise because of our faith in God's provident purpose for it. It would affirm that life finds its meanings and values within a matrix of givens which are themselves gifts and means of grace. And it asserts that man's invested powers of rational self-understanding, moral self-direction, spiritual self-fulfillment are sustained by the self-same love that holds the world in being. It denies that man on his own will ever do better than have his earthly hopes turn ashes—or even when they prosper, to vanish like "snow upon the desert's dusty face." But it affirms that righteousness and love are not merely divine imperatives. They are, in truth, the preconditions of man's true sanity and wholeness.

It is, of course, a commonplace that modern man holds the scales of nuclear life and death for the planet in very unsteady hands.

> Men have brought their powers of subduing the forces of nature to such a pitch that by using them they could now very easily exterminate one another to the last man. They know this—hence arises a great part of their current unrest, their dejection, their mood of apprehension. And now it may be *expected* that the other of the two "heavenly forces," eternal Eros, will put forth his strength so as to maintain himself alongside of his equally immortal adversary [Thanatos].[6]

The date of this eschatological pronouncement was *1930*—and yet it sounds like a prescient comment on the current negotiations for a non-proliferation treaty or a justification for that "hot line" between Washington and Moscow. Of course, the reference to an intervention from "eternal Eros" and his struggle with Thanatos does sound odd—but, after all, Freud was pre-Bultmann and, in that sense, not quite "modern."

Who, then, *is* for humanity? Moreover, who has the heavier burden of credulity in viewing the human prospect? Who is hoping more against hope? Whose morality

6. Freud, *op. cit.*, p. 144. Italics added.

of knowledge is the more scrupulous and unself-righteous? Is it really the case that the Christian tradition is *in essence* antithetical to the maturation and fulfillment of humanity? And, is it true that the anthropology of modern disbelief is more valid than the orthodox account—more authentically human and humane, in either its short- or long-range prospects? Are theological narcissism, iconoclasm, and theological novelties really effective reactions against the blight of "religion"? Is the secular city ever likely to be a more fit place for human habitation now that men have forgotten their vision of the *civitas Dei?* What is the *evidence* for this, or for any part of it? How can any of the proposed answers to these questions be verified? Surely, somewhere in the pondering of our fears and hopes it might occur to a really open mind that the current consensus amongst the self-styled "moderns" is really too facile, that the capacity of the Christian tradition to renew its relevance in a world come of age has been underrated, that Christianity's talk of providence is more than a cosmic analogy of Linus's blanket.

The question of where man's real hope lies gets more urgent by the hour. The world is shrinking, the human family is spawning, the resources of technology are doing scarcely more than "breaking even," the pace and pressures of modern living are steadily mounting. None of the problems of becoming human, of being human, or of staying human is by way of being solved for good and all—molecular biology and planetary emigration to the contrary notwithstanding.

We would, therefore, do better (or so it seems to me) to learn to live in the atmosphere of God's grace with the courage provided by his love—the courage to face death daily and to react to disaster without hitting either the panic or the destruct buttons, to labor and love with the confidence that counts on grace as the fulcrum for the levers we have to push and pull in getting the world's work done.

Instead of reading our fear-reactions as clues to an idiot world, we could learn to decode them as reminders of our radical and ungrudging dependence. Faith is not a falling back on God when all else has failed or is failing. It is, rather, accepting our lives from God's hands, it is having and enjoying and taking leave of the whole round of human life in community as beloved children of God—"in knowledge of whom standeth our eternal life, whose service is our perfect freedom." Is there any other final ground, any other imaginable security?

Now that we have gone on and on in this vein for all these pages, it remains to risk further offense to those who feel they have had enough of "affirmation"—by remarking that Christian liturgy and hymnody are more convincing "demonstrations" of the Christian style of life, as far as words go, than lectures and tomes. The apex of the liturgy, of course, is the Eucharist where, in a gathered congregation called to attention before God, the ordinary essentials of our daily life are consecrated and shared in praise of God and for the hallowing of creation. Nor is this merely "celebration." The "Go in peace" at the end is not a magic rune to ward off the evil-eye, nor yet a license to cop out of life's turmoil. Rather, it is the assurance of an inner peace that "the world can neither give nor take away." But there is also the liturgy of Christian song and it, too, testified abundantly to God's provident care. This is especially true of that multitude of muster-roll hymns that call men to confidence and then commission them to service in the world. These are the vitamins of the Christian diet—and in my case at least, what with the sermons I hear and preach, they often have to serve as proteins too. Rightly enough, most of these hymns are set to marching rhythms, which is part of the point (except that marching up and down the aisles can be taken as an easement of the order to march on out into the street and off to the tasks of the church in the world). These "rousers" number in the hundreds: *I Sing the Almighty Power of God* (". . . whose love is ever nigh"), *O God, Our Help in Ages Past, The King of Love My Shepherd Is, He Who Would Valiant Be, God Is My Strong Salvation, Rejoice, Ye Pure in Heart, God of Grace and God of Glory*, etc. I have no single "favorite" in the lot, but there is one that has always seemed to me to manage the useful combination of offense to the literalists and comfort to the imaginative —a ploy that corresponds, in a way, to the audacity and agony of these lectures. It is from the sixteenth century, it is by Joachim of Magdeburg and it is not in many of the mainstream hymnals. It reeks with non-literal cyphers that a sophisticated man has to scrub and decode as he sings. But what is left—and what was all that ever mattered—is a word that still needs hearing by any "modern" man at all aware that life makes room for radical dependence. It is the word that God's grace for the human future is as fully assured as ever it has been in any past or present. It is the word of a Christian poet that what we mean by "providence" is God's invincible love and that what we mean by "faith" is living in that love.

Who puts his trust
In God most just
Hath built his house securely;
He who relies
On Jesus Christ,
Heaven is his most surely:
Then fixed on thee
My trust shall be
For thy truth cannot alter
While mine thou art
Not death's worst smart
Shall make my courage falter.

Though fiercest foes
My course oppose
A dauntless front I'll show them;
My champion thou,
Lord Christ, art now
Who soon shall overthrow them;
And if but thee
I have in me,
With thy good gifts and Spirit,
Nor death nor hell,
I know full well,
Shall hurt me, through thy merit.

I rest me here
Without a fear—
By thee all shall be given
That I can need,
O, Friend indeed,
For this life or for heaven.

O make me true,
My heart renew
My soul and flesh deliver!
Lord, hear my prayer
And, in thy care,
Keep me in peace forever.

Index

Altizer, Thomas J. J., 5, 22-24, 112
Anselm, 10, 29, 40
anthropology, ix, 4, 11, 18, 26, 36, 131
Apocrypha, 61
apologetics, 26, 41, 70
apologist(s), Christian, 7, 39, 67, 80
Aquinas, 40, 65, 89
Arius, 33
Athanasius, 127
atheism, 5, 25, 98, 105
"Christian," 5
Athens, 57, 78
Auden, W. H., 101
Augsburg, "Religious Peace" of (1555), 114
Augustine, St., xii, 49, 54, 64, 85, 86, 88, 89, 94
contuitus, 49
distentiones, 49
expectatio, 49, 126, 127
memoria, 49
time, 49 ff.
Auschwitz, 90
autonomy, 17, 20, 21, 22, 26, 31, 54, 77, 118, 125

Baronius, Caesar, 63
Barth, Karl, 14, 16, 89
Baur, F. C., 12
Bavinck, Herman, 66
Berkouwer, Gerrit, 66
Bible, 4, 14, 24, 70, 71, 91, 122
Blake, William, 24, 115
Bonhoeffer, Dietrich, 4, 20-22, 37
Braun, Johannes, 65
"Bread of the Presence," 61
Brightman, E. S., 90
Brimm, Henry M., xiv
Brunner, Emil, 14
Bruno, Giordano, 112
Bultmann, Rudolf, 18, 19, 20, 70, 130
Bushnell, Horace, 10

Calvin, 15, 89
Cappadocians, 85
Catholicism, 13, 65, 112, 114
causality, 45, 52, 69, 73
Chalcedon, Definition of, 97
charis, 55 f., 61
charisma, 34
Christianity, 3, 4, 6, 7, 8, 11, 12, 16, 18, 23, 24, 57, 77, 112, 114, 115, 116, 118, 122
in crisis, 3-7
Greek, 59
Latin, 86
liberal, 14, 115, 116

Christianity (*continued*)
"the new essence of," 5, 15, 18
patristic, 32
"religionless," 5, 116
style-of-life, x, 111-135
traditional, 10, 18, 22, 25-26, 27, 28, 30, 85, 111, 112, 113, 122
civitas Dei, 64, 131
civitas terrena, 6, 54, 64
Cobb, John, 42
community, 35, 36, 45, 54, 82, 95, 103, 119, 124, 132
Christian, 4, 6, 13, 62-63, 85
consensus fidelium, 29, 122
Constantine, 113
Constantinople, 47
continuity, 73, 81
Cox, Harvey, 64, 116
creation, 27-28, 32, 34, 55, 60, 65, 66, 71, 72, 84, 92, 103, 104, 109, 126, 132
de nihilo, 32, 72
cuius regio, eius religio, 114

demythologizing, 18, 20, 70
destiny, human, 28, 55, 60
determinism and freedom, 47-52
Dewey, John, 11, 12, 13
dignity, human, 23, 58, 97, 106, 117
Donne, John, 123
Dooyeweerd, Herman, 66

Elliott-Binns, L. E., 67
Enlightenment, 7-10, 14
Epicureanism, 58, 84
Eros, 130
eschatology, 15, 126
secular, 9, 117, 119, 122
Eusebius, 63
evil, problem of, x, 62, 83-91, 96, 100, 106, 108
existentialism, 51, 115

faith, ix, x, xii, 12, 14, 15, 20, 22, 26, 30, 32, 63, 71, 73, 78, 80, 103, 104, 107, 108, 123, 132, 133
disbelief, 4, 6, 8, 25, 27, 28, 30, 42, 57, 83, 118, 123, 127, 131
Farrer, Austin, 89, 91
Feuerbach, Ludwig, 5, 12, 116
Fichte, Johann G., 11, 116
fideism, 26, 32, 37
fides quaerens intellectum, 29
field-theory, unified, 36, 40, 71
Flew, Antony, 93
Fortune, 57
Francis, St., 26
freedom, human, 23, 34, 36, 39, 42-45, 47, 48, 49, 50, 51, 54, 56, 58, 72, 73, 74-77, 93, 101, 103, 104, 109, 114, 117, 125, 132
God's, 71, 91, 94, 95, 96
Freud, Sigmund, 15, 58, 115, 116, 120, 121, 130
fundamentalism, 11, 13

Gandhi, 26
Gay, Peter, 7
Gibbon, Edward, 47
Gnostics, 33, 62, 85
God
communion with, 12, 53, 56
"Death of God," 5, 6, 22, 25, 97
deus ex machina, 5, 6, 19, 31-32, 37, 46, 73, 77
forebearance, 95, 103
grace, 26, 30, 31, 55, 56, 61, 65, 66, 71, 72, 76, 80, 86, 88, 89, 92, 94, 95, 96, 98, 104, 109, 125, 128, 131, 132, 133
immanence of, 62, 73, 86
Immanuel, 106
immutability, 85, 89, 96, 100
impassibility, 85, 89, 96, 100
mercy, 14, 80, 95, 96
presence of, ix, x, 24, 26, 27-28, 33, 47, 55, 56, 60, 67, 71, 73, 80, 82, 91, 107, 109
providence of, ix, x, 6, 27, 30,

33, 41, 46, 55, 61, 64, 65, 66, 67, 69, 71, 72, 76, 77, 79, 80, 81, 83, 84, 89, 95, 98, 106, 109, 123, 125, 126, 128, 133
Provident Mystery, 29, 37, 40, 41, 42, 51, 52, 69, 71, 77, 78, 98, 106
reality of, 4, 26, 55
"special providence," 81
transcendence of, 33, 38, 62, 85, 86, 90, 99, 100
Trinity, doctrine of, 4, 33, 98
Gödel, Kurt, 39
Gollwitzer, Hermann, 26
Gospel, 59, 85, 104
grace, 26, 30, 31, 55, 56, 61, 65, 66, 71, 72, 76, 80, 86, 88, 89, 92, 94, 95, 96, 98, 104, 109, 125, 128, 131, 132, 133

Haight-Ashbury, 74
Hamilton, William, 5, 22-23
happiness, 23, 58, 117, 120, 122
Harnack, Adolf, 12
Hartshorne, Charles, 42
Harvey, Van A., 9
Hazelton, Roger, 68
Hegel, G. W. F., 5
Heidegger, Martin, 16, 99, 116
Heisenberg, Werner, 39
Heppe, Heinrich, 65
Herbert of Cherbury, Lord, 116
heresy, heresies, 4, 5, 62, 96, 98
Hick, John, 86, 88, 89, 91, 93
historiography, 29, 63
history, ix, x, 19, 27-28, 31, 33, 42-47, 50, 51, 53, 55, 56, 59, 60, 62, 70, 80, 95, 105, 129
history and freedom, 42-47
Hobbes, Thomas, 116
Hodge, Charles, 66
homo religiosus, 15
hope, 74, 80, 88, 104, 109, 128
humanism, ix, 7, 10, 28, 36, 111, 112, 115, 117, 118, 123, 127
Christian, 5, 11, 129
religious, ix, 9-13, 26
Hume, David, 8, 116

Ingersoll, Robert G., 6
insight, xiii, 29, 35, 44, 49, 74, 75, 76, 80
Irenaeus, St., 86, 93

Jesus Christ, 4, 6, 26, 55, 59, 61, 62, 65, 76, 80, 81, 82, 86, 91, 96, 97, 104, 105, 107, 126
Christology, 26, 98
Christus Victor, 108, 128
Cross, 60, 62, 85, 91, 96
Incarnation, 53, 55, 79, 86, 96
Messiah, 94, 97
Joachim of Magdeburg, xiii, 133
Job, 24, 94
Johansen, Mrs. Keith H., xiv
John of Damascus, 88
Jones, James A., xiii

Kahler, Erich, 121
kairos, 49, 51
Kant, Immanuel, 11, 15, 37, 120
Kelly, Balmer H., xiv
Kierkegaard, Søren, 16
Kuyper, Abraham, 66

Lactantius, 63
Latourette, K. S., 14
Leith, John H., xiv
liberalism, 11, 13, 15, 16, 90
Lonergan Bernard, 42
love, 51, 54, 55, 64, 74, 76, 92, 97, 103, 105, 109, 113, 130,
agape, 34, 55, 62, 80
God's, 4, 11, 53, 78, 81, 82, 83, 92, 97, 105, 126, 128, 131, 133
Luther, Martin, 15, 125

MacKenzie, Ross, xiv
Mann, Thomas, 92, 93
Marcion, 33, 62, 84
Marcus Aurelius, 124
Maritain, Jacques, 115
Markham, Edward, 101
Marx, Karl, 15, 115, 116
Mathews, Shailer, 116
Mazzini, Giuseppe, 116
McCosh, James, 66

McLuhan, Marshall, 101
memory, 45, 49, 74
metanoia, 50
Mill, John Stuart, 99

narcissism, 13, 16, 39
naturalism, 38, 39
nature, x, 19, 28, 31, 33, 34, 36, 37, 39, 42, 45, 47, 54, 55, 62, 70, 72, 78, 80, 86, 95, 101
Niceo-Constantinopolitan Creed, 126-27
Niebuhr, Reinhold, 14, 115, 116
Nietzsche, Friedrich Wilhelm, 10, 116, 124

Ogden, Schubert M., 42
Old Testament, 84, 94
Olympian gods, 57
order, 36, 53, 55, 64, 70, 72, 80, 93
    causal, 39, 73
Origen, 33, 34, 85
orthodoxy, 14, 15, 17, 85, 112
    neo-orthodoxy, 14-17
overbelief, 16, 27, 43, 70, 104

paganism, 7-9, 67, 77, 99, 100
pagans, Enlightenment, 26
    Greek, 59
    Roman, 63
Pannenberg, Wolfhart, 24, 27
pantheism, 4
Paraclete, 60
pardon, 109
Parousia, 95
patripassianism, 98
Paul, St., 57, 74, 123-28
Pantokrator, 33
Pascal, Blaise, 10
philosophia perennis, 16, 113
Pietism, 21, 22
Pike, James A., 22
Platonism, 58, 63, 84
Plotinism, 58, 84
Pollard, William G., 69
process, 36, 53, 64, 70, 72
proginōskō, 61
prognosis, 61
pronoia, 58, 61
prosdekomenon, 127
Protestantism, 10, 13, 25, 65, 89, 112, 114
prothesis, 58, 61, 63
providence, *see* God, providence of
psychology, 36, 74
purpose, 58, 61

Quillian, Joseph D., Jr., xiv

Rauschenbusch, Walter, 115
reason, 14, 16, 42, 58, 113
revelation, 14, 32, 65, 71, 122
religion, 14, 32, 80, 113
righteousness, 92, 105, 109, 130
Ritschl, Albrecht, 10, 16, 115
Robinson, J. A. T., 22
Rousseau, J.-J., 112

Sabellius, 98
saeculum, 64, 113, 123
salvation, 27, 32, 58, 61, 70, 71, 80, 94, 95, 102, 108
Salvianus, 63
Sartre, Jean-Paul, 16, 99, 115, 116
Satan, 24, 63
Schelling, F. W. J., 12
Schleiermacher, Friedrich, 10
science, 9, 10, 36, 37, 38, 69, 72, 80, 90, 112, 117, 119
"Secular City," 6, 54, 65, 116, 131
Septuagint, 61
Servetus, Michael, 112
Shemmael, 93
Sherlock, William, 66
sin, 81, 83, 90, 99, 102
skepticism, 16, 20, 42
Smith, G. B., 116
Smith, Mrs. Wanda W., xiv
Smylie, James H., xiv
Social Gospel, 11, 13, 115
Socrates, 26, 84
soteriology, 32
Spener, Philipp Jacob, 22
Spirit, Holy, 34, 50, 52, 53, 62, 71, 79, 105

spirituality, 62
Sprunt Lectures, ix
Stoics, 58, 59, 63, 71, 84
Stradivarius, Antonio, 90
supernaturalism, 13, 15, 22
Syllabus of Errors, 112

Taylor, Jeremy, 123
technology, 9, 31, 54, 90, 117, 119, 131
Tennyson, Alfred, 17-18
Tertullian, 85
Thanatos, 130
theodicy, 84-91, 98-99
Theodosius II, 47
theologia crucis, x, 99-107
theology, ix, x, 4, 11, 18, 19, 29, 37, 67
  biblical, 95
  contemporary, 10, 98
  "death of God," 22
  radical, ix, 6, 84, 123
  traditional, 5, 32, 33, 86, 99
Thomas, Dylan, 101
Thomas, John N., xiv
Tillich, Paul, 16, 68
Tolstoy, Leo, 46
Torah, 95
tradition, Christian, xii, 17, 28, 53, 55, 56, 80, 96, 131
"two natures," 4, 12

Union Theological Seminary, Richmond, Virginia, ix, xiii-xiv

Van Buren, Paul, 26
Vatican II, 13, 112
Voltaire, 7, 8, 99, 111
  Ecrasez l'infâme, 7, 122

Wesley, John, 8, 22
White, James A., xiv
Whitehead, A. N., 58, 72
Winkworth, Catherine, xiii